HOW·TO·WIN·AT
VIDEO GAMES
A COMPLETE GUIDE

HOW·TO·WIN·AT
VIDEO GAMES
A COMPLETE GUIDE

GEORGE SULLIVAN

SCHOLASTIC BOOK SERVICES
New York Toronto London Auckland Sydney Tokyo

ISBN 0-590-32630-9

Text copyright © 1982 by George Sullivan. Illustrations copyright © 1982 by Margo Hrubec. Published by Scholastic Book Services, a division of Scholastic Inc.

12 11 10 9 8 7 6 5 4 3 2 1   9   2 3 4 5 6/8

Printed in the U.S.A.   01

Many people helped the author by disclosing the strategy and tactics that have enabled them to master certain video games. Special thanks are due Billie Billing (who provided the charts relating to Pac-Man, as well as other information), Justin Bua, Tim Sullivan, John Devaney, and Luke Devaney.

Contents _____

Chapter 1

KA-BOOM...
GRONK...
BLEEP-BLIP

You drop a quarter in the slot, rest one finger on the fire button, and grasp the control knob with your other hand. The screen comes alive with squiggly, glowing monsters, with enemy space-ships that attack in waves, or ferocious robots that seek to destroy everything in their paths.

For the next few minutes, the computer in this electronic video game is going to do everything in its power to wipe you out.

Your fingers flick the controls this way and that. You know your tank, spaceship, or hero will be de-stroyed in the blink of an eye if you don't make the right moves.

You hardly notice the sounds that blare from the machine—*ka-boom . . . gronk . . . c-r-r-unch . . . bleep-blip.*

This scene is repeated millions of times each day

across America. If the game isn't Centipede or Asteroids, it's Berzerk or Pac-Man. Fans of all ages play regularly.

Games are found in arcades, supermarkets, airports, restaurants, movie lobbies, gas stations, pizza parlors, and candy stores. There are machines at the Y.M.C.A. in Grand Rapids, Michigan; a record shop in Skokie, Illinois; and the basement of the dining center at Haverford College in Haverford, Pennsylvania.

The games have chalked up some startling statistics. In one year recently, an estimated $2.8 billion was pumped into them. At a quarter a game, that means that some 11.2 billion games were played, an average of almost 50 games for every man, woman, and child in America.

How do you explain this popularity? Noted science writer Isaac Asimov says this: "Kids like the computer because it plays back. You can play with it, but it is completely under your control. It's a pal, a friend, but it doesn't get mad. It doesn't say, 'I won't play,' and it doesn't break the rules. What kid wouldn't want that?"

There's a lot more to video games than just having fun. You just don't sit and watch, as you do with TV or the movies. You're a participant. You plan and execute strategy. The games do a great deal to develop hand–eye coordination.

Some educators say that the games help improve other practical skills. Because game players learn to focus on an entire screen of beep-beeping flying objects, they may become faster readers and better drivers.

There are emotional benefits, too. A game can give a person a sense of accomplishment, even a sense of mastery.

Of course, not everyone looks upon the games as the greatest invention since home television. Some parents worry that their children spend too much time and money on the games.

Overuse *can* be a serious problem. "If a kid keys on games as the main reason for living," says one psychiatrist, "then he's got real trouble."

Actually, there are three types of video games. The most popular type is the coin-operated game, found in arcades.

Gaining fast in popularity are the game units that attach to home TV sets.

Table models and hand-held games are the third type. Some of these are no bigger than a deck of playing cards.

No matter which type of game you enjoy, this book is meant to help you. It tells you how games work. It offers some history. There are tips that can make you a better player. There's advice you can put to use when buying a game. There's even a video game quiz. There's no book on the subject that's more complete.

How the Games Work

Your efforts to master video games are likely to be made a bit easier if you come to understand what makes them tick. The information given in this section won't enable you to build a game of your own, but at least you'll get some idea of what your quarters are paying for.

Electronic video games are made up of three basic elements: a video screen, a simple control panel, and a series of computer chips that are designed to produce the images that appear on the screen.

The video screen is something like the screen of your home television set. It has been designed to accept the video images sent out by the chips.

The chips are the heart of every video game. Each chip is a tiny circuit board, smaller than the tip of your little finger. Made of silicon, the chip combines transistors, resistors, diodes, and other electronic parts.

A modern video game may require six ROM 32-K chips, each of which handles 32,000 bits of information. ROM means *read only memory*. A ROM chip is permanently programmed. It stores the rules of the game, the point values, and other such information that never changes.

RAM chips handle information of a temporary nature: your score, the day's high scores, and the number of spaceships or laser bases you have remaining. RAM means *random access memory*.

Each chip is designed to produce one or more images common to the game being played. In Pac-Man, for instance, there are chips that draw the board outline and its dividers, creating the pathways. There are chips that produce the image of Pac-Man himself; chips that draw the dots, energizers, and fruit; and chips that draw the monsters and regulate their movement.

All of the chips are connected to a circuit board that enables them to "talk" to one another. The vital part of the circuit board is a master chip that controls the system and all of its components. The master chip is called a microprocessor.

The microprocessor is actually a tiny computer that processes information according to the way in which the computer has been programmed. The microprocessor that controls the Pac-Man game makes the monsters pursue Pac-Man, produces the dots to be gobbled up, produces the energizers, keeps score, keeps track of the screen you're playing, and registers each of Pac-Man's deaths. It controls each fragment of sound you hear. But that same microprocessor, if programmed with a different set of instructions, could do your mathematics homework or keep an accurate inventory of your record collection.

When you step up to the Pac-Man machine, put in your quarter, and shove the control stick in one direction or another, you're actually giving a signal to the microprocessor. The microprocessor relays your command to the Pac-Man chip. The Pac-Man chip then redraws Pac-Man black—the color of the screen's background—making him disappear. It also establishes Pac-Man's new position according to your instructions and then draws him there in yellow.

The sequence in which Pac-Man is made to disappear and is redrawn happens every time you move Pac-Man. But it happens so fast—30 times a second—that to you, the player, Pac-Man appears to be moving. The microprocessor common to many video games performs more calculations in one second than earlier computers could perform in many hours.

The next time you see a video game, think of the waves of color that dazzle your eyes and the sounds that crash about your ears as being bursts of information. And bear in mind that each line and each piece of sound is being controlled by the game's magical microprocessor.

Before You Begin

If you're a beginner, spend some time getting acquainted with the games at your local arcade. Every game has a control panel. In some, the controls are simple. Playing Pac-Man, for instance, requires only the use of a control rod, called a joystick. Move it to the left, Pac-Man scampers to the left; move it to the right, Pac-Man heads right.

With other machines, the controls are more complex. In Defender, you handle an up–down lever, a reverse button, a thrust button, a fire button, and also buttons that control a smart bomb and a hyperspace feature. It may look as if there are controls enough to pilot a DC-10. But don't worry; with experience (and the tips provided later in this book), you can tame even Defender.

No matter which game you play, you always have the same goal: to score points. Scoring points usually involves destroying enemy missiles or alien invaders. In Pac-Man, however, you try to gobble up monsters who are out to devour *you*. In Donkey Kong, the idea is to save a young lady who has been kidnapped by a gorilla. There's a game to suit just about every taste.

Most games have a fire button as well as some type of directional control. After you've gotten your spaceship, airplane, tank, or laser base properly lined up, you press the fire button to send a missile, bomb, rocket, or bullet on its way. A direct hit usually causes the enemy craft to explode or disappear.

Once you've cleared the screen of enemies, another screen appears, one more difficult than the first. Screens are also called waves, rounds, attacks, missions, boards, or sectors. You play until the enemies destroy you.

Before you spend a single quarter, survey the games at your local arcade. Decide on a type of game that you'll enjoy. It's easier to become skilled at a game you like.

There are four different categories of games. They are:

Shoot-and-Run You have only two control systems to worry about on games of this type. One of them moves your spaceship or control center to the right or left, and up or down. The other, either a fire button or a trigger, enables you to destroy the attacking enemy. You fire, then quickly flee to avoid the enemy's counterfire.

Space Invaders is a typical game of the shoot-and-run type. Others include Astro-Blaster, Astro-Fighter, Centipede, Devil Zone, Galaxian, Gorf, Moon Shuttle, Phoenix, Pleiades, and Radar Scope.

In Outer Space In games of this type, you're at the controls of a sophisticated space vehicle. You have buttons or a joystick that controls the ship's direction and a thrust button that sends your spaceship zooming ahead. You have a fire button that enables you to blast away at the enemy.

Games in this category often have a hyperspace button, too. Press it and your ship disappears from the screen, but quickly materializes again in some random spot. There may also be a shield button that enables you to protect your ship in emergency situations.

Games of this type include Asteroids, Defender, Ripoff, Space Fury, Space Odyssey, and Star Castle.

Maze Games Some game-players never have anything to do with alien invaders or hyperspace buttons. Asteroids and laser beams are unknown to them. These people are maze-game players.

Pac-Man is the best-known game of this type. Using the joystick, you move Pac-Man through a network of interconnecting pathways as he seeks to avoid being eaten by four hungry monsters.

Most other maze games include a firing button which gives you the power to eliminate your enemies. There are many different maze games, including Amidar, Armor Attack, Armored Car, Berzerk, Frenzy, Frogger, Make Trax, Mouse Trap, Space Panic, Targ, Tranquilizer, Venture, and Wizard of Wor.

Reflex-Action Games Imagine you're at the wheel of a speeding race car, one foot on the gas pedal and one hand at the gearshift. Sometimes the road ahead is pocked with potholes. Other times dangerous wet spots appear. You have to wrestle with the steering wheel to keep in control.

You also have to watch out for other cars that stray across the road in front of you and occasionally go rebounding off roadside barriers. Another hazard is an ambulance that keeps coming up behind your vehicle. You'd better swerve to get out of the way!

This is Monaco GP, a typical reflex-action game. You're the driver of a racing car moving at full tilt. Your score depends on how well and how quickly you react to the many perils you're made to face.

In the reflex-action games called Sky Raider and Scramble, you're at the controls of an airplane hurtling through the sky. And in Space Zap, the scene shifts to outer space. Other reflex-action games include Grand Champion, Rally X, Super Cobra, and Turbo.

No matter what type of game you choose, there are certain tried and proven playing methods you should follow that will help to make you a superior player. The chapter that follows discusses them.

Chapter 2

HOW TO BECOME SKILLED

Video games challenge you. They never stop. At first you will lose badly. But little by little, you'll improve. It takes skill, common sense, and patience.

It also takes quarters, pocketfuls of them. This chapter tells you how to increase your knowledge and sharpen your skills, advice that's meant to save you quarters.

BECOME AN OBSERVER

Once you've chosen a game you think you're going to like, watch others play it before you try. But just don't watch anyone. Pick out a superior player.

Watch like a hawk. Imagine that you're the player, and think how you would be acting and reacting if your hands were on the controls.

As you watch, say nothing at all. The arcade itself may be ten times noisier than your school lunchroom, but you yourself must be a silent observer.

You might, however, want to utter a word or two of praise should the player accomplish something that is truly spectacular. "Nice move," you can say.

If possible, get the expert to give you a few tips about the game. That's a very quick way to learn. It may even be worthwhile to provide the expert's quarters for two or three plays. You'll save money in the long run.

READ THE GAME INSTRUCTIONS

Just to the right or left of the screen, there's a small panel that tells how the game is scored (and not much else). This information is important. It's likely to affect the strategy you use. For example, in Centipede, shooting the scorpion is worth a bonus of 1,000 points. The scorpion is the richest target in the game. This means that whenever the scorpion appears, you should put forth extra effort to destroy it.

Some targets are always more important than others. That applies to every game, not just Centipede. Be certain you know all of the game's point values before you play.

CONCENTRATE

When you play a video game, you enter another world. Every ounce of your energy should be concentrated on what's happening in that world. You can't sip a soft drink. Forget about potato chips and other snacks. If a friend says "Hi," return the greeting when the game has ended. If you're not going to concentrate, spend your quarter on a candy bar.

DEVELOP QUICK HANDS

The best players are those who have learned to process the visual information the game presents and translate it into rapid finger movements. Pickpockets and third basemen should excel as game players.

How do you develop quickness? Ping-Pong will help; if you don't have anyone to play with, simply try hitting a Ping-Pong ball off a wall.

You can also improve your quickness with this drill: Place a quarter in your right hand and close your fingers about it. Standing erect, stretch your arm straight out in front of you, the back of the hand facing the ceiling. Keep your arm parallel to the floor.

Now open your fingers, letting the quarter drop. Catch it with the same hand before it hits the floor. Gradually increase the distance you allow the quarter to drop.

When you've mastered the drill with your right hand, try it with your left. You may be surprised at how fast you become skilled.

MASTER THE GAME'S TEMPO

Every game operates according to certain set patterns established by its program. This makes for a certain rhythm in the movement of objects on the screen. In Space Invaders and other games of that type, there's a stop-shoot-run rhythm involved in destroying the enemy aliens. In Asteroids and other space vehicle games, you rely on a thrust-turn-shoot rhythm.

If the game has a fire button, determine exactly how it fires. In Missile Command, each of the game's three fire buttons sends missiles into the air in rapid succession, one right after the other. But in Phoenix, when you press the fire button, there's a pause—a split-second delay—before the missile blasts into the air.

Try to establish the tempo of every game you play.

PRACTICE, PRACTICE, PRACTICE

Ed Logg is the name of the man who dreamed up most of the electronic wizardry that went into Asteroids, the very popular and imaginative arcade game. People ask him all the time, "What is the secret of Asteroids?"

Logg always gives the same answer. "Just play a lot," he says. "That's the secret. It takes a lot of practice."

That's true. Whether it's Asteroids or any other

game, you have to practice. Unless you practice, you can't expect to ever be a star.

But it has to be the right kind of practice. The wrong kind wastes quarters.

When you practice, don't merely play your favorite game over and over. Sure, that will help you. But you'll improve at a much faster rate if you practice key skills.

A tennis player who wants to improve doesn't merely play tennis. He or she may spend long hours working on just one shot—hitting backhands by the hundreds, for instance. Or slamming one overhead after another until he or she becomes arm-weary.

Apply that same kind of thinking to your favorite video game. For example:

• In Space Invaders, practice the shoot-and-dodge technique that enables you to kill invaders as quickly as possible while avoiding their missiles.

• In Pac-Man, practice using the tunnel to outmaneuver the monsters.

• In Asteroids, spend time learning how to control your spaceship. Notice how most of the experienced players can flip the ship around the screen, sending it exactly where they want it to go. Learn how to use the rotate buttons first, then the thrust button. Then learn to use a rotate button and the thrust button at the same time so that you can turn the ship as it soars.

Whenever you spend time practicing a key skill,

your overall score for the game is likely to suffer. That can't be helped. But in the long run, this method of practice will help to boost your scores quicker than any other.

EXPERIMENT

Almost every video game program uses a *random event generator*, or REG. The REG causes enemy tanks, missiles, lasers, or other objects to appear without any definite pattern. You have to keep alert every second. The REG also prevents you from knowing in advance the point value of the next object you're going to destroy.

Once in a while, however, you may get the feeling that the appearances of various objects, or their point values, are not occurring at random. Instead, there seems to be a definite pattern to them. In such cases, you might want to experiment to see whether you can determine the pattern.

If your experiment is a success, it can pay rich dividends. The best known case of successful experimentation involves Space Invaders. One feature of Space Invaders is the small flying saucer that flits across the top of the screen from time to time. Not long after Space Invaders was introduced, players came to realize that by destroying the flying saucer at certain times, a bonus of 300 points could be earned. At other times, wiping out the saucer was worth only 50, 100, or 150 points.

At first, it was generally believed that these point values were determined by an REG, that they occurred at random. Experimentation proved otherwise. It was established that destroying the flying saucer earns 300 points when it is hit on the twenty-third shot of every screen and on every fifteenth shot thereafter. (That's why Space Invaders enthusiasts are shot counters.)

Other games may have patterns that are similar to those found in Space Invaders. By experimenting, you may be able to find them.

MEMORIZE

Some games do not have any REGs at all. Much of what happens fits patterns that never change.

Maze games and reflex-action games are usually of this type. To excel in these, you should memorize the patterns common to each. In Pac-Man, study the layout of the maze pathways and memorize where the entrances and exits have been placed. In Scramble, study the placement of the enemy rockets and fuel tanks and how the flying saucers array themselves as they attack. These things never change.

Write down important numbers, positions, and movements in a small notebook. Or work with a partner who makes notes while you play. Once you've memorized your observations, you'll have the mastery of the game within your reach.

BE CONFIDENT

Don't try to overwhelm the game the first few times you play. That's the secret of gaining confidence.

Set goals that are realistic. They should challenge you, but not be impossible to reach. When playing Pac-Man, for instance, set a goal of clearing the first board, the first screen. If you're a beginner, that won't be easy. But with some experience, you'll do it. You'll get a real sense of accomplishment when it happens the first time. Your confidence will grow.

Then raise your goals. Try clearing two screens, then three. Or set goals in terms of point totals, maybe 10,000 points at first, then 20,000, or 25,000.

You don't become confident overnight. There's a building process involved.

COMPLAIN AND EXPLAIN

Suppose you've practiced your favorite game by the hour, you've learned to observe and you've learned to concentrate, and your hands are so quick that you're thinking of becoming a magician—and your scores are still an embarrassment to you. What then? Should you admit that you simply lack the necessary skills? Not at all. Instead, develop several excuses that you can rely upon. Here are some from which to choose:

- "I wasn't playing for score—I was just experimenting."

- "The stick (or knob, or firing button, or trigger, or whatever) is too loose (or too tight). There's no way to control the game."

- "Never talk to me when I'm playing. You see what you made me do!"

- "I thought they fixed this machine" (said through clenched teeth and while wearing a scowl).

- "Somebody bumped into me."

- "I can't stand it when someone stares at the screen when I'm playing. It makes me lose my concentration."

- "There must be a new chip in this machine. It never played like this before."

- "I never get a break."

A final word: In your struggle against the games, never feel that you are overmatched. Quite the opposite is true, in fact. You, the player, always have the upper hand. This is because the computer must always do what it has been told to do. The computer cannot think for itself (even though it sometimes might appear otherwise). However, you can; you can use your intelligence and imagination to experiment and vary your play and outwit the computer. You always have the edge.

Chapter 3

SECRETS OF BEATING THE GAMES

This chapter offers step-by-step strategy that will help you to outsmart fourteen of the most popular video games. In the chapter after this one, the strategy and tactics for beating Pac-Man are given.

Once you develop skill in playing a particular game, don't feel you have it beaten for all time. Machines can be adjusted to make them more difficult. Some, in fact, have several levels of difficulty. Thus, you may find that a machine on which you once scored very well now skins you alive. It won't always happen, but you should be prepared in case it does.

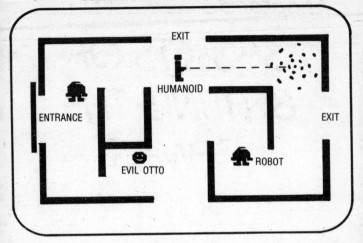

BERZERK

In this popular maze game you control a humanoid, a tiny stick figure who shoots from the hip as he seeks to outduel and outmaneuver a gang of killer robots. Despite its rough-and-tumble theme, Berzerk is a game with a sense of humor. When you run out of the maze with the robots chasing you, the machine's voice cries out, "Chicken! Fight like a robot!" And when a game ends, the machine shows it has a shrewd commercial sense by announcing, "Coin detected in pocket."

How the Game Is Played

Each game begins with you, the humanoid, posted at one of the four edges of the maze. Then your enemies, the robots, appear. There can be as few as four of them or as many as twelve. You try to weave your way through the maze, escaping by means of an exit at the opposite end. Touching any wall means death.

The robots fire at you continuously, and you fire at them. While you have the ability to move in each of eight different directions, the robots can match you step for step. Besides firing deadly bullets, they can also cause your death by colliding with you.

Then there is an Evil Otto, a bouncing ball that wears a fixed grin. Otto, who makes his appearance about ten seconds after the game has begun, is on the side of the robots. He pursues the humanoid by bouncing after him. If there are still robots on the screen when Otto appears, he bounces along at a relatively slow pace. But should all of the robots have been eliminated, Otto hops at a rapid clip. When Otto touches the humanoid, he destroys him.

You'll often complete a maze in a bit more or less than fifteen seconds. Another will be instantly thrown up on the screen. There are said to be 64,000 different maze combinations in this game, so don't bother attempting to memorize maze patterns.

Controls

You control the humanoid with an eight-directional joystick. The joystick also serves to aim the humanoid's pistol. As this suggests, you cannot send the humanoid running in one direction and have him fire in another. As he goes, so does he shoot.

You tap a firing button with the fingers of your other hand. You can fire at the rate of about two bullets a second.

Scoring

You earn 50 points for each robot you destroy and a bonus of 10 points per robot when you destroy all the robots in any particular maze.

After you've accumulated 5,000 points, you earn a bonus of another humanoid.

Strategy and Tactics

- The opening seconds of each maze are critical. The humanoid always appears first, then the robots. Within one second after their appearance, the robots start firing. Even good players can be wiped out at the beginning—unless they remember to take aim and start firing immediately.

  Figure out in advance on which side of the maze the humanoid is going to appear. It's always the one opposite the side where he made his exit. If he exited at the top of the maze, he'll appear at the bottom.

- Should one or more robots open fire on you just

as the game opens, resist the impulse to dodge by backing into the wall behind you. That wall, like all the others, causes death. Instead, duck to the right, left, or diagonally—and keep shooting.

- The robots may be deadly, but they are also dim-witted. You can often get them to make dumb mistakes. Suppose you're on one side of a wall, and a robot is on the other. Walk toward the end of the wall. The robot will do the same. Just as he emerges from behind the wall, pick him off. In the same manner, you can sometimes lure a robot into walking into a wall, which of course is fatal to him also.

  Or try this: Suppose two robots are on the other side of a wall from you and close to one another. Scurry back and forth rapidly. The robots are likely to get so confused that they will collide, destroying each other.

  Other times you're likely to find yourself in between two robots, both of whom fire at you. Step out of the way and let the bullets go by. You can guess the results.

  You can also use Otto to wipe out a robot or two. When Otto appears, he immediately heads for you. If there happens to be a robot in the center of the maze, lure Otto toward the center. He'll zap the robot before he gets near you. And you'll get the points.

- It's much more difficult to deal with robots in a

cluster. Bullets come at you from several different directions. If possible, dart behind a wall for protection.

If no wall is near, put some distance between yourself and the robots, then start firing back. The farther away you are from your enemies, the better your chances of dodging their bullets.

- When you shoot a robot, he explodes. Be careful about being too close to a robot when you fire. You can also die in the explosion.

- Know your enemy. The robots each have a different amount of firepower, depending upon their color. In the original version of Berzerk, the breakdown is as follows:

  Yellow robots have *no* bullets (but can destroy the humanoid by colliding with him).

  Red robots shoot *one* bullet at a time.

  White robots shoot *two* bullets at a time.

- Diagonal shots are the hardest to dodge. If you have a choice of robots to shoot, first destroy the one that requires diagonal shots. You will thus avoid being the target of his diagonal fire.

- After your score reaches 5,000 points, Otto's speed doubles. You can't delay for a split second when he appears. You've got to take flight.

- Remember, you don't have to destroy all of the robots in a maze. You can often escape by fleeing through the maze exit.

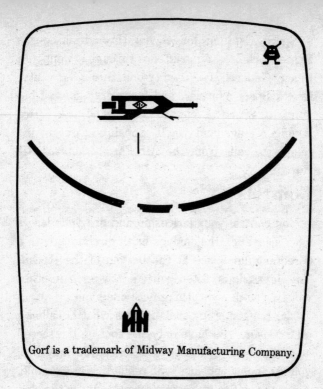

Gorf is a trademark of Midway Manufacturing Company.

GORF

This is not merely one game, but five of them in one package. In each game, your spaceship is the target. Fortunately, the various missiles that are fired in your direction are not guided missiles. They drop like World War II bombs, which means you can dodge them.

Once you've battled your way through the five missions, they're repeated at a more difficult level. For the first five missions, you're designated a Space Cadet; for missions six through ten, you're a Space Captain; for eleven through fifteen, a Space Colonel; for sixteen through twenty, a Space General; for twenty-one through twenty-five, a Space Warrior, and for twenty-six and beyond, a Space Avenger. Go beyond the Space Avenger stage and you'll probably start getting telephone calls from the Air Force (the *real* Air Force).

Controls

You control your spaceship and fire your lasers with a joystick that moves in all directions within a rectangular space at the bottom of the screen. The joystick is fitted with a trigger. In other words, you do everything with one hand.

The trigger is unusual. It fires what is called a quark laser. You have only one shot on the screen at a time, but of the several shots you may fire, you decide which one will remain. For example, suppose you fire at the enemy and you see the shot is going to miss. Simply pull the trigger again. Not only do you send a new laser on its way, but you cancel the first shot. It disappears from the screen.

This feature is not the same as rapid-fire. Continuous pulling of the trigger is almost valueless in this game.

It's vital to learn how to control your spaceship smoothly and easily. The first few times you play this game, concentrate on developing a sense of how fast the ship moves in response to your commands. Also get into the habit of evaluating each of your shots, so you can fire again as soon as you realize one is off target.

The pages that follow list the various point values, plus the strategies and tactics, common to each of the five Gorfian missions.

Astro Battles

If you're good at Space Invaders, you'll be a star in Astro Battles. While the two games are very similar, Astro Battles is the easier of the two.

As this game opens, a robot appears at the right side of the screen and begins dropping aliens in a rectangular pattern. The rectangle becomes eight rows across, with three aliens to a row. Shooting an alien is worth 100 points.

You can also shoot the robot, which is worth 250 points. As the game proceeds, other flying robots appear from time to time. They are worth 300 points apiece.

Once the aliens are in formation, they begin their familiar lockstep movement, marching first to the right side of the screen, then to the left, then back and forth, back and forth. To pick them off, use the same shoot-and-run technique common to Space Invaders. (It will help you to read the section on Space Invaders in this book.) Fire your laser, then quickly dart to the right or left, avoiding enemy fire. Then dart back, take another shot, and speed away again.

You're protected to some extent by a force field, a white semicircular band about a quarter of an inch in width that extends from one side of the screen to the other. It plays much the same role as the shelters do in Space Invaders. The enemy missiles cannot penetrate it at first; they must blast holes in it. But sections of the force field magically disappear to allow your shots to pass through.

When you destroy a robot within the rectangle in which your ship is assigned to operate, the point value you receive is displayed on the screen for a second or two. Beware of these numerals. Touch them with your ship and it will be destroyed.

Once your ship has been eliminated, whether by collision with numerals or through enemy fire, the screen ends. This thought should make you very much of a defensive player. Never take any unnecessary risks.

Laser Attack

This time you come under attack from two laser cannons which are flanked by a host of escorts that resemble bumblebees. The cannons dance up and down and shift from side to side, always accompanied by their escorts. Each cannon stops only long enough to emit deadly laser blasts which take the form of long needle-thin flashes of bright yellow light.

Every few seconds, one or two of the escorts breaks away from the pack to dive down in an attempt to destroy your spaceship by colliding with it. If you fail to destroy an escort, but do manage to dodge it, the escort rejoins its colleagues at the top of the screen, and awaits the command to attack again.

Your mission is to destroy the cannons and all of their escorts. While you should always try to bring down an escort attacker, your first goal should be to destroy the cannons. Use the same strategy you used in shooting the enemy aliens in the previous screen. Dart underneath a cannon, fire, then scamper away. You have to be especially careful in attacking the first cannon because the other will be firing at you. Once the cannons have been destroyed, it's not difficult to finish off the escorts.

Galaxians

This screen offers a variation of the game Galaxian (see page 70), but instead of facing 46 enemy warriors, you're confronted with only 24 of them. As the round opens, they're arranged in four rows: two rows of eight, a row of six, and a row of two. A Gorfian robot drifts across the top of the screen from time to time. Destroy the robot and you earn 100 points.

Every few seconds, a Galaxian breaks away from the right or left edge of the cluster and sweeps down toward your ship, sending pellet-shaped bombs in your direction and attempting to collide with you from the side.

Stay low, firing as frequently as possible into the Galaxian formation. As it shifts to the right, you should shift, too. When the cluster goes back, go with it.

Keeping low is important. Not only does it give you greater opportunity to avoid the Galaxians' bombs, but you can zoom upward and escape whenever you're threatened with an attack from the side.

Space Warp

This is the most imaginative of the rounds. A black disc about the size of a quarter appears at the center of the screen. Dozens of brightly colored lines radiate from it. Spaceships and bomb-tossing Gorfian robots come spiraling out of the disc one at a time. They balloon in size as they travel. Each will be destroyed by your laser or fly off the edge of the screen—or destroy you. For each one you hit, you earn 100 points.

Keep your eyes on the disc so you'll know exactly when an enemy ship appears and the direction in which it is going to be traveling. Keep your own ship higher on the screen than usual, and blast away at the disc. Shift from side to side to avoid enemy fire.

In later rounds, attackers emerge from the disc at much faster speeds. You'll be forced to revise your strategy, retreating more toward the bottom of the screen to avoid collisions.

A string of dots appears just inside the outer edge of the disc. It serves as a counter. Whenever an enemy ship emerges from the disc, one dot of the string disappears. Keep track of the dots. When they're all gone, the round ends.

Flagship

Looking like a vehicle out of Star Wars, the flagship soars across the top of the screen, descending once in each crossing to drop deadly diamond-shaped bombs. You must place a shot dead center in the nuclear reactor to destroy the flagship. The ship then explodes in a dazzling visual display; you earn 1,000 points and get advanced in rank. Then the next round begins.

When one of your lasers hits the ship at some spot other than the reactor, you get 20 points. Keep plugging away until you blast a chunk of metal from the ship, and you earn 150 points.

A force field similar to the one in the first round, except that it is inverted, protects the flagship. Your shots will be blocked by the force field until you blast some holes in it. But it offers you not the slightest bit of protection. Bombs from the flagship pass right through it.

Begin by blasting off chunks of the flagship. Then go for the reactor.

There are two places of safety for your ship— either of the upper corners of the screen. You're out of the flagship's range of fire when you take refuge there.

When you reach this screen in the later rounds, two Gorfian robots ride on top of the flagship. Destroy them first if you can. Otherwise, they'll fly down in an attempt to collide with your ship, distracting you in your effort to put the flagship out of commission.

FROGGER

Frogger is a fast-paced game with an easy control system. You have to steer a frog safely through two mazes and do it within a certain amount of time. If you like beating the clock, you should enjoy Frogger.

How the Game Is Played

The screen for Frogger is made up of two maze-like sections, one on top of the other. The bottom half is a multilane highway, bristling with automobiles, wide-tired dune buggies, farm vehicles, and big trucks. The top half is a river with groups of turtles, logs that go floating by, and an occasional crocodile. A stone wall separates the highway and the river. Sometimes there are hungry snakes on top of the wall.

The idea is to lead the frog across the highway, over the wall, over the river (this frog does not swim; he'll drown if he falls in the water), and have him hop to safety into one of the five docks at the top of the screen. As you can imagine, one hazard after another confronts the poor frog. There's the heavy traffic on the highway. Some of the turtles sink when he hops upon them. Otters lurk in the river waiting to gobble him up, and when he seeks refuge on a log, it may turn out to be a crocodile.

All the while, a timer at the bottom of the

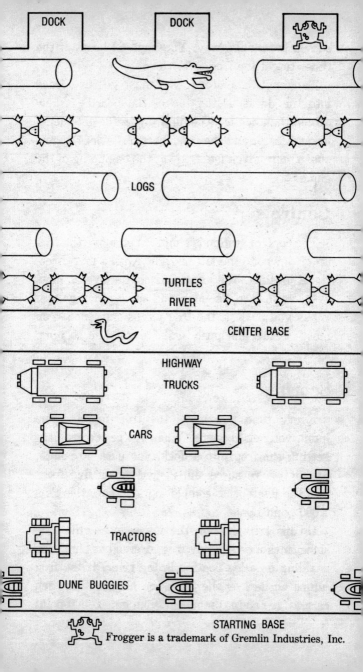

screen is ticking away. You have 60 beats of the timer to get the frog safely home.

To complete a board, you must get five frogs into the docks at the top of the board. A new screen then begins. The highway traffic gets heavier and faster and the river becomes more dangerous. You're given five frogs at the beginning of the game.

Controls

The control system is simple. You move the frog up or down, to the left or right, with a four-directional joystick. The joystick is not automatic, however, as it is in Pac-Man and some other games. When you push it, the frog jumps only once. You must release and push again to get him to jump again.

Scoring

Every time you move the frog forward one jump, you get 10 points. When you're successful in getting the frog into a dock, you earn 50 points. And if you're successful in getting all five frogs into the five docks, completing a screen, there's a 1,000-point bonus.

On his trip through the upper maze, the frog sometimes meets a lady frog, dressed in pink. She is riding on a log floating in the river. If the frog jumps on her, or she jumps on him, and he then carries her into the dock, you get a 200-point bonus.

The frog may encounter insects at the dock. Eating an insect is also worth 200 points.

As mentioned above, the timer is ticking away, 60 beats to a screen. For every beat that remains on the timer when the frog reaches the safety of the dock, you earn 10 points.

When you've accumulated 20,000 points, you're given a bonus of an extra frog.

Strategy and Tactics

- Be a bit cautious at the beginning. There's no need to rush out onto that busy highway. If the frog is only brushed by a vehicle, it's the end of him. Wait for a gap in the traffic. Or move the frog to the right or left, to where a gap is to be found.

- The highway and the river are not the only hazards the frog faces. You can cause his death by missing a dock when you attempt to jump into it, by jumping into a dock already occupied by a frog, by floating off an edge of the screen while riding a log or turtle, or, of course, by running out of time.

- Don't worry about the time element in the early screens. There's no need to rush. You'll find it takes only from 30 to 40 beats to lead the frog through the mazes to the dock.

  Many beginners are in a hurry. The frog is

destroyed on the highway or drowns in the river. Be patient. Wait for gaps to occur.

- Turtles can change in color from red to green. They also change in size. Beware of turtles that change to green and get smaller. A frog seeking to ride such a turtle will drown.

- Of the five docks, the most difficult to enter is the one on the extreme left. The frog must be maneuvered to the left of the dock in order to be able to jump into it, but there are few opportunities to do this.

  The trick is to put the frog aboard a turtle in the second row from the top and ride to the left. Then, just before reaching the edge of the screen, jump onto a log and then quickly into the dock.

  If you're guilty of a misjudgment and no log appears, simply jump back onto a log that's moving to the right to avoid colliding with the edge of the screen. Then try again.

SPACE INVADERS

At one time not many years ago, the video game industry was gripped with Space Invaders fever. The game was the Pac-Man of its day. Although its popularity has faded, Space Invaders still collects quarters in good numbers.

How the Game Is Played

On the face of it, Space Invaders is simple. From your laser base, you seek to destroy fifty-five alien invaders, which are grouped in eleven columns, five invaders to a column. When you accomplish this, a second and more determined screen of invaders appears, then a third, a fourth, and so on.

The invaders move sideways until they reach an edge of the screen, and then the formation drops one level and begins moving in the opposite direction. In the first screen, the invaders drop eleven levels. On the second round, they start one level lower, reaching the bottom after dropping ten levels. On each succeeding screen, they start another level lower.

You're given three laser bases at the beginning of a game. When your laser base is hit by an enemy missile, it is destroyed. When you lose all three of your bases or any of the invaders reaches the bottom row, the game ends.

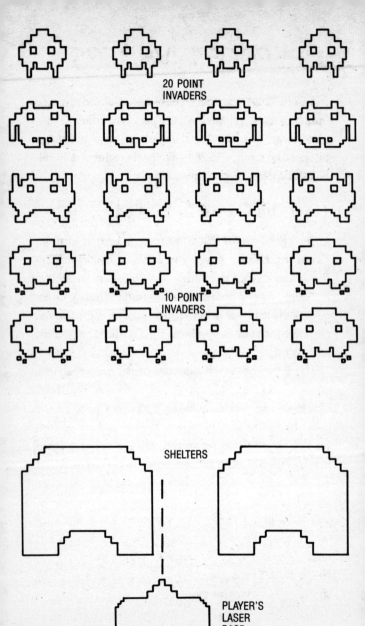

20 POINT
INVADERS

10 POINT
INVADERS

SHELTERS

PLAYER'S
LASER
BASE

Space Invaders is a trademark of Taito America Corporation.

Controls

In early models of this game, pushbuttons were used to move the laser base from right to left and back. Nowadays you control the movement of the base with a joystick. There is also a firing button.

Scoring

Picking off invaders is worth from 10 to 30 points. Those in the first two rows from the bottom earn you 10 points; those in the third and fourth rows, 20 points; and those in the last row (the top row), 30 points.

Occasionally a UFO floats by at the top of the screen. Destroying the UFO can earn 50, 100, 150, or 300 points. As a beginner, don't worry about the UFO. You'll have your hands full defending against the advancing aliens.

Strategy and Tactics

- Understand your weapon—your laser. Once it is fired, you cannot shoot it again until one of the following takes place:

  Your shot hits an invader.

  Your shot hits a shelter.

  Your shot is destroyed.

  Your shot reaches the top of the screen.

  Always keep one eye on each of your shots to determine where it ends. Then take your next shot as quickly as possible.

- At the bottom of the screen are four shelters, which can be used to protect your laser base. Little by little these shelters are destroyed by the invaders' missiles and by your own laser shots.

  You can dart out from the safety of a shelter, fire, and then dart back to escape the missile fire. Or you can park beneath a shelter with just enough of your base protruding to give you an unobstructed shot. You can also blast a hole through the center of a shelter and then fire away.

- Come out shooting! Your laser base first appears at the lower left corner of the screen. Nudge it to the right so as to be able to destroy the third column of invaders. One shot should follow another as rapidly as the machine permits you to fire.

  When you've completely destroyed the third column, slide your laser base to the left and start shooting the invaders in the second column. Next, destroy column one.

  The alien force is now only eight columns wide (consisting of columns four through eleven). You've created a zone on the left side of the screen where you can take refuge from enemy missiles.

  Now move your laser base to the extreme right of the screen, and destroy column eleven.

  The invaders keep dropping lower and lower.

Moving your laser from right to left, wipe out the bottom row.

Return to the right side of the screen and destroy column ten. Then pick off the bottom row. There are now eighteen invaders remaining, a cluster of six columns, three invaders to a column.

Shoot down the column of invaders farthest to the left. Then destroy the bottom row. Now ten invaders remain, two rows of five invaders each. Shoot them two by two.

- By the time you've played Space Invaders a few times, you should have developed a shoot-run-shoot-run technique. You fire, dart to the right or left to avoid the oncoming missile, then dart back to fire at the next higher invader in the column and flee again. Once you've achieved this rhythm, you're on your way to good scores.

- When a laser shot and missile collide in midair, they usually destroy one another. Sometimes, however, the missile survives the collision, and it continues in its death-dealing course. A laser shot never survives.

- The speed with which the invaders move from side to side varies with their numbers. At the beginning of the round, they move with relative slowness. As you begin destroying them, the speed of the survivors increases. After you've blasted the forty-seventh invader from the screen and only eight are left, their speed jumps dramatically.

When there's only one surviving invader, he scurries back and forth at headlong speed. And he's spewing out missiles almost continually. He's a very dangerous little guy.

But notice that his speed from right to left is a bit slower than from left to right. It's easier to pick him off when he's moving in that direction, to the left. Park your laser base near the left side of the screen. As he approaches, start firing.

- The UFOs that soar across the top of the screen move first from left to right, then from right to left. After you've destroyed forty-six of the invaders and only nine remain, no more UFOs appear.

To assure that you nail the UFOs that are worth 300 points, you must count your shots. It's possible to bring down eight 300-point UFOs during the first screen. That's 2,400 points, an enormous number. By comparison, realize that if you destroy every one of the 55 invaders, you earn only 990 points.

To earn the 300-point bonus, you must shoot the UFO on your twenty-third shot and on every fifteenth shot thereafter.

Six 300-point UFOs appear during the second rack and four during the third screen. On succeeding screens, the invaders start so low on the screen and reach the bottom so quickly, it's not likely you'll have time to be concerned with UFOs.

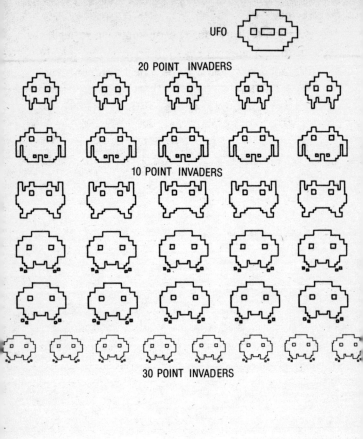

UFO

20 POINT INVADERS

10 POINT INVADERS

30 POINT INVADERS

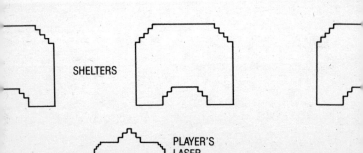

SHELTERS

PLAYER'S
LASER
BASE

Space Invaders II is a trademark of Taito America Corporation.

SPACE INVADERS II

While this game is very similar to the original Space Invaders, it offers a number of new features. The most unusual involves some of the invaders. When hit, they divide into small reproductions of the original invaders. These "new" twins immediately begin flitting back and forth, dropping bombs.

Another innovation is a flying saucer that blinks on and off as it travels from right to left. You're able to destroy it only when it's visible, that is, when it has blinked on.

This blinking UFO can perform in an unusual manner. From the third round on it drops reinforcements, in the form of fresh invaders, into the top row. This is a frustrating piece of strategy for anyone nearing completion of a screen.

While these new features may prove troublesome, if you get high scores in the original Space Invaders, you'll also do well in this version.

How the Game Is Played

Same as Space Invaders

Controls

Same as for Space Invaders

Scoring

Same as in Space Invaders, but with these additions: You earn 30 points for destroying any invader that divides in two and 200 points for wiping out a flashing UFO.

The scoreboard can now record as many as 99,990 points, not merely 9,990. And when you get one of the day's high scores, you sign in with ten letters, not three.

Strategy and Tactics

- The methods used in destroying the invaders that are described in the previous section of this book also apply to this version of the game. Destroy the first three columns and also column eleven. Keep following the instructions until you've cleared the screen.

  The fact that some invaders split in two will force you to be a bit more cautious, however. The smaller invaders are difficult targets, although they actually grow and shrink as the game continues, so they're not small all of the time.

  You'll make your task easier if you remember to pick off the splitting invaders two at a time. This strategy yields not four, but only three, replacements.

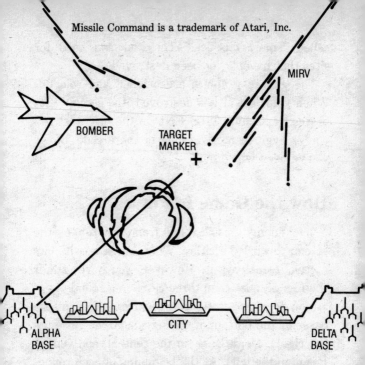

Missile Command is a trademark of Atari, Inc.

MIRV

BOMBER

TARGET
MARKER
+

ALPHA
BASE

CITY

DELTA
BASE

MISSILE COMMAND

Your mission in this game is to protect six cities by destroying enemy missiles, bombers, and satellites with missiles of your own. As long as one of your cities survives, the game continues.

Missile Command begins at a reasonable pace and it is not altogether difficult to keep matters under control. But it builds in stages to a fast and furious level. Pause only long enough to scratch an ear, and you'll lose a city or two.

Not only do the enemy missiles get faster and more accurate, but you have to cope with what are

57

called "smart missiles." These always head for sites that haven't yet been destroyed.

The game's graphics are original and colorful. When your last city is destroyed, the screen celebrates by flashing THE END in the brightest red you've ever seen. Everyone in the arcade knows you've been wiped out.

How the Game Is Played

The enemy missiles fall from the top of the screen toward the cities. Whenever a missile hits a city, it destroys it. However, you never suffer the loss of more than three cities in a round.

You do your counterattacking from three missile bases at the bottom of the screen: Alpha Base (on the right), Delta Base (in the center), and Omega Base (on the left). At the beginning of each round, each base is equipped with 10 missiles.

You aim your missiles by means of a target mark that has the shape of a plus sign (+). You put the plus sign where you want it by spinning a trak ball. You then press a fire button to launch the missile.

The explosion that results fills an area about the size of a golf ball. Any enemy missile, satellite, or bomber that comes in contact with the cloud is destroyed. Although it takes only about a second for the missile cloud to shrink into nothingness, it's possible to have as many as eight clouds on the screen at the same time.

Controls

Besides the trak ball, which is somewhat larger than the ball used in Centipede, and which you use to control your target mark, you have three fire buttons, one for each missile base. Missiles launched from Delta Base travel faster than those from the other two bases.

Scoring

You earn 25 points for each attack missile you destroy, 100 points for each bomber, 100 points for each killer satellite, and 125 for each smart missile.

In addition, you get bonus points at the end of each round: 5 points for each unused missile in your arsenal and 100 points for each city that remains.

After the second round, the point values begin to balloon in size. In rounds three and four, every score, including the bonuses, is multiplied by two; in the fifth and sixth rounds, by three; in the seventh and eighth rounds, by four; in the ninth and tenth rounds, by five; and in all rounds that follow, by six.

With every 10,000 points you score, you receive a bonus city. You need bonus cities because cities can get wiped out very fast once the smart missiles start falling.

Strategy and Tactics

- The secret of success in this game is being fast and precise in controlling your target mark, the plus sign (+). Being fast means putting the mark where you want it—hitting one of the fire buttons—and then moving on. Never wait around to see the results of your shot. You'll find out soon enough. It's always fire-and-fly-away, fire-and-fly-away.

  You become precise with the trak ball through practice. You should be able to put the plus sign exactly where you want it without even thinking. It should be almost a reflex action.

- You must aim in front of a missile to bring it down. Whenever possible launch your missiles from Alpha Base or Omega Base, whichever is closest to the target. Save the faster Delta missiles for emergencies.

- Since the number of missiles you have in your arsenal is limited (ten per base), it's usually best to press only one fire button at a time.

- Destroy bombers and satellites as soon as you can. It will save you from having to deal with the missiles they are going to launch.

- Develop the strategy of saturation bombing to wipe out heavy fire. This strategy is also known as "making a wall." As soon as the round begins, position your target mark just below the center on one side of the screen. Then start moving it straight across the screen toward the other side, pressing the fire button eight times as you go. If you're moving the target mark from left to right, fire from Omega Base. If you're going from right to left, fire from Alpha Base.

You'll leave a string of eight golf-ball–sized explosions in your wake. This will absorb most of the enemy fire. But a few missiles may trickle through. Pick them off with fire from Delta Base.

- In most rounds enemy fire is launched in two waves. After making a wall to destroy the first wave, repeat the process to wipe out the second wave. The second wall of fire should be laid down in the other direction, using the base in the opposite corner. You should still have enough firepower in Delta Base to deal with any enemy missiles that survive.

- The first smart missile appears in round six. You'll recognize it by its diamond shape. It can head for any city that has not been destroyed, unless you have already lost three cities. As stated above, you can never lose more than three cities in a round.

You have to fire with greater accuracy when seeking to destroy a smart missile. The ordinary missile will be wiped out by merely touching the cloud of destruction created by your missile. But a smart missile can dodge any defensive missile that explodes a quarter of an inch or more below it.

Your chance of success in attempting to destroy a smart missile will increase if you remember to use a quick missile from Delta Base. Wait until the smart missile is nearing ground level, then position your target mark just below it, and fire.

- The fact that the game continues for as long as one city survives gives rise to a strategy you can use to build an enormous point total. In the game's later rounds, when the pace becomes frantic, don't bother trying to protect more than one city. This enables you to concentrate on the many smart missiles that will be launched. The points you earn from destroying just these smart missiles will be enough to earn you a bonus city.

- After you've destroyed the last enemy missile of a round, you'll hear a distinctive beep, and your target mark (the plus sign) will vanish from the screen, not to reappear until the next round begins. If you destroy what you think was the last missile of the round, but you don't hear a beep and the target mark remains visible, keep alert—more missiles are on the way.

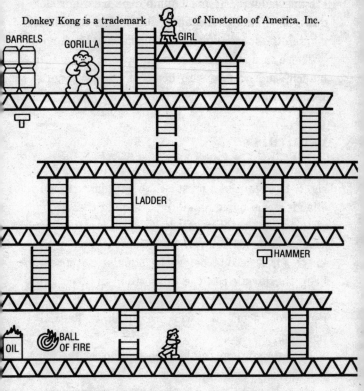

Donkey Kong is a trademark of Nintendo of America, Inc.

BARRELS
GORILLA
GIRL
LADDER
HAMMER
OIL
BALL OF FIRE

DONKEY KONG

You get a chance to be a hero in this game. A helpless young lady has been kidnapped by a gorilla. He is holding her captive at the top of an unfinished skyscraper.

Your mission is to guide a plump little man in a hard hat safely to the top of the structure where he makes the rescue. As the hero climbs the girders and ladders, he must jump over barrels rolled down at him by the ape. The higher the hero climbs, the more difficult the challenges become.

There are no bullets to fire, no rockets to launch, and no lasers to beam at enemy targets. Donkey Kong is just plain fun.

Controls

You move the hero up or down, or to the left or right, by means of a joystick. To get him to ascend a ladder, you move him into position at the bottom of it and push the joystick forward. As the hero reaches the next level, he is on his hands and knees for a second before he stands. Be sure to keep the joystick in the up position until he gets to his feet. If you happen to move it to the left or right too soon, he will freeze in a kneeling position.

How do you get the hero to jump over the barrels the ape tosses in his direction? You do it with a jump button. You use the button so frequently that the hero of this game is called Jumpman.

Jumpman can be made to jump any time he is standing still or moving to his left or right. The distance he can leap is equal to the distance of one of his walking steps. He cannot be made to jump when he is moving either up or down.

You often use the joystick and the jump button at the same time. Shift the joystick to the left and press the jump button, and Jumpman will leap to his left, hurtling any barrel or other hazard that threatens to do him in.

Sometimes it's necessary to make Jumpman leap straight up into the air and come down in the same spot. All you have to do is adjust the joystick to its neutral position, then press the jump button.

You may find that you're able to do your best when you control the joystick with your right hand (even though it's positioned on the left side of the console) and press the jump button with your left hand (although it's on the right side of the console). This means that when you're using both controls, you'll be cross-handed. Nevertheless, many players prefer this method, and find it makes for the highest scores.

Scoring

At the beginning of each round, you're given a bonus of from 5,000 to 8,000 points. As you attempt to navigate Jumpman to the top of the skyscraper, the point total starts melting away at the rate of 100 points every two or three seconds.

When Jumpman leaps over a barrel or other obstacle, you get 100 points. Hitting a barrel with a hammer that is sometimes available to Jumpman is worth from 300 to 800 points.

At various times during the game, the girl's umbrella, her hat, and her purse appear at random locations on the screen. When Jumpman passes over any of these objects, a bonus of 300 to 800 points is awarded.

You're given three lives for Jumpman at the beginning of the game. You get a bonus Jumpman when your point total reaches 12,000 points.

How the Game Is Played

In the opening seconds of the game, the plot unfolds. Kong carries the young lady to the top of an unfinished building. Jumpman appears at the lower left-hand corner of the screen. Kong begins rolling barrels down at him. Fireballs are another threat. Any time a barrel or a fireball comes in contact with Jumpman, it's curtains for him.

When you're successful in getting Jumpman to the top of the skyscraper, the gorilla tucks his victim under one arm and climbs to a higher floor. A new round begins. The plot is the same but the obstacles that Jumpman faces are different. There are four different screens, with two or more levels of difficulty for each of them.

Strategy and Tactics

- Timing is all important in this game, no matter which screen you happen to be playing. You have to size up what's happening and then move Jumpman accordingly. Sometimes it's best not to move him at all, but simply play a waiting game. For example, suppose you start Jumpman up a ladder, but as he nears the top you notice that a series of barrels is rolling toward him. Simply hold him in position on the ladder until the barrels thunder past. You should use this type of strategy frequently.

- In the first round, concentrate on getting Jumpman to the top of the skyscraper as quickly as possible. The ladders at the center of the screen offer the quickest route.

- Despite what's said above, sometimes it's better for Jumpman to destroy a barrel rather than attempt to avoid it or leap over it. Two hammers hang at different levels of the sky- scraper, and Jumpman can use either one to destroy the barrels. To pick up a hammer, move Jumpman near to it and then jump.

  Hammers can cause problems, however. Once Jumpman has a hammer in his hand, he is no longer able to ascend, descend, or jump. When a hammer begins to flash a different color, it's a signal it's about to disappear.

- Partial or broken ladders sometimes appear. These can provide Jumpman with a temporary refuge when barrels come careening toward him. Simply have him climb down one of these ladders until the barrel passes overhead. Don't allow him to go beyond the last rung, however. That will prove fatal.

- In the second round, you're presented with several more stories of skyscraper framework. Within the flooring of each story, there are two widely separated openings that have been fitted with plugs. Jumpman knocks out a plug by running or jumping over it. The object of this round is to dislodge all of the plugs. Once that has been accomplished, the building collapses and Kong plunges headfirst to the ground. End of screen.

Once a plug has been removed, the resulting opening has to be avoided. Jumpman must leap over it. If he fails to do so say bye-bye to him.

- Those gaps in the floor aren't the only hazard in the second screen. Jumpman is also imperiled by a series of fireballs. The fireballs tend to cluster anywhere a plug remains in place.

  Despite their scary appearance, the fireballs have a timid nature. When you bring Jumpman face to face with a fireball, the fireball will retreat. But beware of attacks from the rear.

- The third screen is more hectic than any of the others. There are both stationary platforms and moving platforms arranged between the top and bottom floors of the skyscraper. There are also several ladders. Fireballs keep skipping down from the top level, and there are bouncing hammers that also must be avoided.

  To get to the top, Jumpman can either hop aboard an ascending platform or climb a series of ladders. Again, timing is a key factor. Station Jumpman on a platform where you know he will be protected from the fireballs, then move him upward when the danger has passed.

As for the bouncing hammers, notice that they always bounce in the same spots. And after bouncing three times, they fall straight down. Once you've figured out how the hammers move, you'll find it much easier to avoid them.

- In the fourth screen, you're inside what appears to be a pie factory. Pies, which menace Jumpman, are moving to and fro on conveyor belts. Jumpman must also avoid fireballs and a barrel of boiling oil that's positioned in the center of the screen.

Despite all of the hazards, this is not a difficult board. The structure has only four levels. You must get Jumpman to the top level. Ladders connect the levels. Sometimes, however, the ladders are incomplete and thus hazardous. The trick is to wait for a "good" ladder (one that safely connects two levels) and then have Jumpman ascend it.

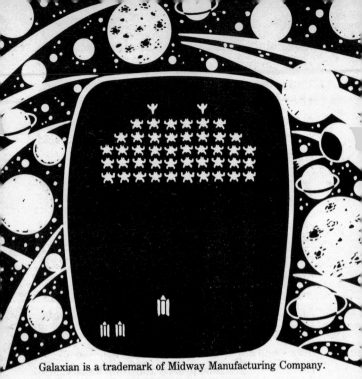

Galaxian is a trademark of Midway Manufacturing Company.

GALAXIAN

This game is similar to Space Invaders, but there's more action to it. Again you're pitted against a formation of alien invaders constantly shifting from one side of the screen to the other. But instead of remaining in even columns, these invaders can peel off from the group and swoop down toward your spaceship, littering the landscape with bombs. You not only have to shoot-and-dodge, but now the aliens you're dodging are looping through the sky. Still, Galaxian is not a difficult game. Not long after it was introduced, the manufacturer began developing a successor to it, a game that was similar but offered a greater challenge.

How the Game Is Played

There are forty-six Galaxians on the screen at the start of the game, ten in each of the three bottom rows, eight in the next row, six in the next, and two mystery Galaxians in the top row.

At frequent intervals, a Galaxian from the right or left edge of the formation breaks off from the pack and zooms down toward your spaceship, dropping needle-shaped bombs. If you fail to destroy an alien during his bombing run, he exits at the bottom of the screen, then reappears at the top to rejoin the formation.

Your spaceship can be destroyed by a collision with the Galaxians as well as by the bombs they drop. You're given three spaceships at the beginning of the game.

Small flags in the lower right corner of the board identify the screen being played. One flag means the first screen, three flags the third screen, seven flags the seventh screen, and so on.

The later screens are made more difficult by increasing the number of Galaxians and sending as many as five of them on attack at once. And the attackers cover a much wider area of the screen on each bombing sweep.

Controls

You have directional buttons that control the side-to-side movement of your ship. You also have a fire button. There's no rapid-fire, however. You have only one missile on the screen at a time. In other words, the next missile won't appear until the previous one explodes.

Scoring

Each alien has two point values, one when it is destroyed in formation, and another—double the amount of the first—when it is destroyed while attacking. The blue Galaxian is worth 30 points when destroyed in formation and 60 points when attacking; the purple Galaxian, 40 points in formation, 80 points attacking; and the red Galaxian, 50 points in formation, 100 points attacking.

In addition, there are mystery Galaxians, each of which has four different point values. If you destroy a mystery Galaxian when it attacks alone, it is worth 150 points; when attacking with an escort, 200 points; with two escorts, 300 points. If you nail both escorts before destroying the Galaxian, you get 800 points.

Strategy and Tactics

- This is basically a shoot-and-run game. Keep firing as rapidly as the firing button allows. As you fire, shift to the left or right with the Galaxian formation so as not to waste shots.

- Always keep an eye on the attackers' bombs, and be ready to dodge them. This holds true even after you've destroyed an attacker. His bombs can still destroy you.

- Study the Galaxians' attack patterns to determine the point at which each is the easiest target. The purple Galaxians, for example, always fly horizontally across the screen and then reverse direction with a lazy turn. It's during this turn that they're the most vulnerable.

- When you fail to destroy an attacker, or when there are so many attackers on the screen that you're overwhelmed by them, you may be able to take refuge at the left or right edges of the screen. This is true, however, only during the early screens.

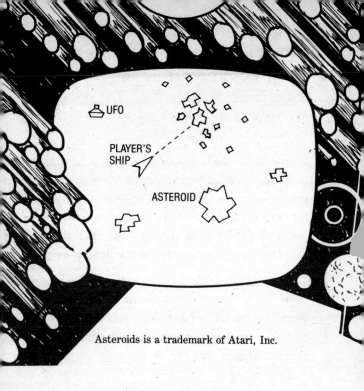

Asteroids is a trademark of Atari, Inc.

ASTEROIDS

Like Space Invaders, Asteroids once ranked as the most popular game in the universe, then other games overtook it. But during 1982, Asteroids made a comeback with a model that offered a giant screen. This enables performances to be viewed by a good-sized number of spectators. Skilled performers thus get a chance to show off. If you're a beginner you'll no doubt want to stick with the original version of the game on its screen of standard size. Since Asteroids still has fans by the millions, there are plenty of machines around.

How the Game Is Played

You're an astronaut in outer space, controlling a small triangular-shaped spaceship in free flight. The ship can rotate 360 degrees and zoom at different speeds in all directions. Your task is to dodge various chunks of space rubble that drift toward your spaceship or blast away at them. You also must fend off enemy flying saucers that appear from time to time.

You start with a fleet of three ships, which you operate one at a time. The game continues until your last ship has either collided with an asteroid or been destroyed in a shootout with a saucer.

When play begins, your ship appears in the center of the screen. Four big asteroids—many players call them rocks—materialize near the borders of the screen and begin to move in random patterns and at random speeds, but generally they drift toward your spaceship.

When a large asteroid is struck by one of your shots or a shot from a flying saucer, or it collides with a flying saucer, it divides into medium-sized asteroids. Each medium-sized asteroid divides into two smaller ones. The speed and direction of the asteroid fragments tend to differ from that of the "mother" asteroid.

There are two sizes of flying saucers, large and

small. They both originate on either the right or left side of the screen.

The second screen introduces six large asteroids, and the third screen, eight of them. All succeeding screens consist of ten large asteroids.

Controls

You control the spaceship with five white pushbuttons. The ship's direction is controlled by a rotate-right or a rotate-left button. A thrust button propels the ship forward. You use the fire button to send missiles on their way.

The hyperspace button is unusual. When you push it, the spaceship vanishes, then reappears in an empty section of the screen. You use hyperspace in very tight spots, when destruction of the ship seems certain.

Scoring

Large asteroids are worth 20 points; medium asteroids, 50 points; and small asteroids, 100 points. The large UFO earns you 200 points, and the small UFO, 1,000 points.

For every 10,000 points you earn, you win an extra spaceship.

Strategy and Tactics

- Achieving pinpoint control with your spaceship is the key to success in this game. First, learn to use the rotate buttons, one of which spins the ship to the left, the other to the right.

Then learn to use the thrust button in combination with one of the rotate buttons, sending the ship through the sky on a controlled journey.

Stopping the soaring ship will be a problem, at least at first. There's no brake; there's no retro rocket. You stop by making a 180-degree turn while tapping the thrust button. This has the same effect as firing a retro rocket.

Once you've learned to control the spaceship, you can aim it like a pistol before you fire. You'll also be able to dodge asteroids, flying saucers, and the missiles the saucers fire.

● Your spaceship can fire up to four missiles at a time. Once these four shots have been fired, you can't shoot again until one of them hits something or simply dies of old age.

When you start a screen, fire in frequent bursts of two shots. It's risky firing three or four times in a burst, because you might not have any missiles left should an emergency occur.

● If you're moving forward when you fire, your missiles travel faster than they do when you are standing still. If you are moving backward, they travel more slowly.

● The large UFOs fire at random. But the

smaller ones know where you are and the direction in which you're traveling. They pick out a target area slightly larger than your spaceship, and fire randomly toward it. For this reason you should never move straight toward any of the smaller saucers. Doing so makes you a bigger target. The farther you are from a saucer, the smaller the target you offer.

- The higher your score, the more accurate the smaller saucers become.

- Any object that disappears off one side of the screen reappears at the corresponding point on the other side. You can thus sometimes destroy an asteroid or a saucer by firing *away* from it. The saucers cannot do this. Even when a saucer has a good chance of hitting you by firing off the side, it will fire toward the center of the screen.

- Whenever one of your spaceships is destroyed, the new one will appear at the center of the screen. It will be positioned at exactly the same firing angle as the ship that was destroyed.

- Experienced players are very wary about using the hyperspace button. Not only can your ship reappear at a hazardous spot on the screen, but there is approximately one chance in five that your ship will blow up on reentry. In other words, hitting the hyperspace button is something like playing Russian roulette.

Nevertheless, there will be times you'll find a missile bearing down on you, and there's no chance of escape. The hyperspace button is the only solution.

- Lurking is the strategy to use if your goal is to get a big score. Pick off all of the asteroids, except for one small or medium asteroid. Then lie in ambush near one of the edges of the screen, waiting for a small saucer to appear.

  If it appears on the side where you're lurking, fire quickly and destroy it before it can get off a shot. If the saucer appears on the side opposite you, take advantage of the game's wraparound feature, fire off the screen away from the saucer, thus blasting it from behind.

  You can keep doing this until you accidentally destroy the remaining asteroid (which causes a new screen to appear), or collide with a saucer. Advanced players have been known to simply abandon the game out of boredom.

- A variation of this strategy calls for you to again eliminate all of the asteroids but one. Then, keeping your spaceship pointing toward the middle of the screen, propel it from the bottom to the top, reentering the screen at the bottom. Then surge toward the top of the screen again. Keep doing this over and over. Whenever a flying saucer appears, turn and blast away at it.

  Thus, you'll be moving in a continuous vertical line. If you're able to avoid colliding with the asteroid or getting wiped out by a saucer, the game can last indefinitely.

- If your favorite Asteroids machine seems faster than usual one day, it may be because the arcade owner has had a new chip installed to speed things up. The chip can increase the speed of all moving objects on the screen, including your spaceship and its missiles by as much as 50 percent.

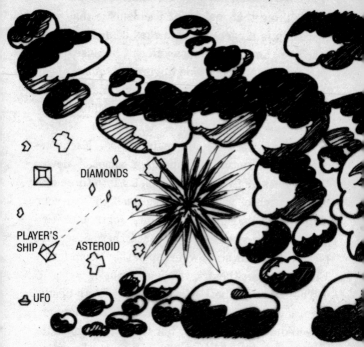

DIAMONDS

PLAYER'S
SHIP

ASTEROID

UFO

ASTEROIDS DELUXE

"It's a tough game to beat." That was the comment of one young player, a master at the original Asteroids, after giving Asteroids Deluxe a few tries. Many arcaders agree with this comment. In fact, in the first few months after Asteroids Deluxe was introduced, it proved so difficult that many players turned their backs on the machine. Now, thanks to a new microchip, it's not quite as difficult as it once was.

One thing that makes for problems is that your spaceship is bigger, which makes it an easier target. The game is also more difficult because of the introduction of a four-sided figure—a square about the size of a cough drop—that has many of the same characteristics as an asteroid. Collide with a square and your spaceship is destroyed.

The square causes other problems. Each one drifts about until you ram it or shoot it down. When you shoot it, the square splits into three diamonds, each of which launches itself toward your ship. Each diamond, when hit, splits into two wedges. The wedges rotate until their noses are pointing at your ship, whereupon they zoom for it. Either you get them, or they get you.

The larger of the UFOs now shoots with deadly accuracy. Three out of every four of its shots are directed at the asteroids, but the fourth heads for your spaceship. The smaller UFO is also more deadly. It fires at the asteroids only once out of every two shots it takes; the other, of course, is directed at your ship.

The first screen contains six of the larger asteroids. (The number is four in the original game.) No screen ever begins with more than nine of the larger asteroids. (The number can reach as high as sixteen in the original game.)

How the Game Is Played

Same as Asteroids

Controls

Much the same as in Asteroids. But instead of the hyperspace feature, you now have a shield button at your control. This puts a wall of protection between your ship and the oncoming asteroids, squares, diamonds, or wedges. When shielded, your ship cannot be destroyed by a collision. But the asteroid, square, diamond, or wedge can be destroyed by your shielded ship. So can a UFO.

The shield is not perfect, however. While a shielded spaceship can rotate and be propelled in one direction or another by means of the thrust button, it cannot shoot. And the shield does not protect your ship should it come under attack by any two objects—a pair of asteroids, a pair of wedges, an asteroid and a square, or any other such combination.

In addition to these failings, the protection of the shield lasts only a few seconds. Once it runs out, you cannot use the shield again until the next screen.

Scoring

Same as Asteroids, with these additions: Destroying a square is worth 50 points; a diamond, 100 points; and a wedge, 200 points.

Strategy and Tactics

- The screen's outer edges are not as well defined as in the original Asteroids game. Objects hovering near the edges appear to be out of focus. Keep your spaceship away from the edges, because you may not be able to spot an asteroid, square, or UFO until it is too late.

- When a square appears, avoid it by maneuvering your spaceship until the end of the round. If you shoot a square early in the round, you'll have to face the attacking diamonds and then the wedges.

- The UFOs shoot with far greater accuracy in this version of the game. Their shots are going to explode asteroids and, even worse, squares. Be prepared to face the attacks that are going to result.

- Use the spaceship shield only in an emergency, or when there is an obvious tactical advantage. For example, your ship may be only a cornflake's width away from a UFO. That's a perfect time to press the shield button and ram the attacker, finishing him off.

CENTIPEDE

The panel that bears the instructions for Centipede contains these two sentences: "Shoot to destroy advancing creatures for points," and "Collisions with any creatures will destroy you." While those two sentences accurately summarize what takes place, they give no hint of how frantic this game is. It seethes with activity. You can't relax long enough to blink your eyes. Little wonder that Centipede ranked as one of the most popular games of all during 1982.

How the Game Is Played

Spiders, fleas, scorpions, and centipedes—all residents of a crowded mushroom patch—are your enemies. When the game begins, a centipede made up of a head and eleven body segments (resembling a string of beads) appears at the top of the screen and begins to weave its way down through the rows of mushrooms.

Your goal is to destroy the centipede. Once you do so, the second round begins. This time there are two centipedes. One has a head and ten body segments, the other only a head.

In the third round, you are faced with a nine-segment centipede and two heads. And so it goes until the twelfth round, when you must cope with twelve heads. After the twelfth round, the entire sequence is repeated.

Centipede is a trademark of Atari, Inc.

MUSHROOMS

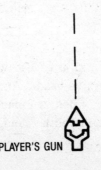

LONG
CENTIPEDE

PLAYER'S GUN

You're given three guns at the beginning of each round. Each time a centipede, flea, spider, or scorpion collides with a gun, the gun is destroyed.

Controls

The position of your gun is controlled by a trak ball, a plastic sphere about the size of a tennis ball, which is partially recessed in the game console. The gun moves in whichever direction you spin the ball.

Many players use their fingertips to spin the ball. But you're likely to find that you can achieve greater control if you use the middle parts of your fingers. When you use your fingertips, you're not able to move your gun smoothly and at a controlled speed. Using the middle of the fingers gives you this control.

You also control a fire button. Your gun spews out only one bullet at a time. But when you hold the button down, you assure that the next bullet will fire as soon as the one previous has hit its target or has traveled to the top of the screen. This gives a rapid-fire effect whenever a target is close.

The gun fires only straight upward. Its movement is limited to a zone that extends across the bottom of the screen and this is about three inches from top to bottom.

Scoring

For destroying a centipede's head, you earn 100

points; destroying one of the centipede's body segments is worth 10 points.

Other point values are as follows:

- Mushroom: 1 point (must be totally destroyed)
- Flea: 200 points
- Spider: 300, 600, or 900 points (depending on its distance from the gun; the closer the spider, the higher the score)
- Scorpion: 1,000 points

When your gun is destroyed, you receive 5 bonus points for each partially destroyed mushroom and each poisonous mushroom. The mushrooms are restored to their normal state before the next screen begins.

Every time you accumulate 12,000 points, you receive a bonus gun.

Strategy and Tactics

- You should be constantly on the move, flitting from left to right, as you pick off centipede segments and mushrooms. It's vital to keep the player's zone clear of mushrooms. Mushrooms can attract centipedes, and the centipedes can destroy you.

  While you want to keep the gun positioned within or as close as possible to the bottom row of the player's zone, you also want to get as close as possible to whatever target you have lined up. This gives you rapid-fire capability.

- When you shoot a centipede in the head, the head turns into a mushroom. The next segment in the chain of segments that makes up the centipede then becomes the head.

  When one of your shots hits one of the centipede's body segments, that segment becomes a mushroom. The centipede then splits into two parts. The tail section grows a head. The two parts then begin moving in opposite directions.

  Always try to destroy a centipede before it divides into smaller parts. Move your gun into position beneath the spot where you expect the centipede to turn. When the centipede's head is directly above your gun, start firing. You'll thereby destroy the head and turn it into a mushroom; the mushroom will also be destroyed.

  As the next segment in the string turns into a mushroom, it, too, will be destroyed—and so on down the line. For each segment you destroy, you earn 100 points.

- When a centipede divides into smaller segments, try this strategy: Aim your gun at the tail segment. Holding the fire button down, spin the trak ball so the gun sweeps from the tail to the head. Although you earn only 10 points for each segment you destroy, the mushrooms you create will serve as a barrier, preventing the centipede from turning toward you.

- Rapid-fire is not recommended in every situation. It is often best to keep tapping the fire button, instead of holding it down. With rapid-fire you lose control. You may be confronted with a situation where you're not able to fire when you have to.

• Different methods are required for dealing with each of the other inhabitants of the mushroom patch:

Fleas You don't start seeing fleas until the beginning of the second round. They drop down one at a time from the top of the screen whenever fewer than five mushrooms remain in the player's zone. As they descend, they leave a trail of mushrooms behind.

Fleas are not a serious threat unless your gun happens to be directly under one as it falls and you fail to shoot. Nevertheless, try to destroy the fleas before they enter your zone. Doing so not only earns you points, but also saves you the trouble of clearing up the mushrooms they leave behind. Don't use rapid-fire, however. You must have at least one shot in reserve to destroy the occasional flea that comes plunging directly toward you.

Spiders Popping onto the screen from one of the upper corners of the player's zone, the spider bounces up and down like a rubber ball, caroming off the top and bottom edges of the zone and any centipedes or mushrooms that happen to be in it. Any mushrooms touched by the spider are erased, but you receive no points for them. Because of its erratic movement, the spider is a constant danger.

Shoot the spider if you're not too busy shooting centipedes. It's a rich source of points. If you're unable to shoot it, at least dodge it. The spider always makes its exit on the opposite side of the zone from which it enters. If the spider enters the zone at the upper right-hand corner, and you wish to dodge it, quickly shift the gun to the right side. You'll be safe there since the spider will go bouncing toward the left side.

Scorpions With a 1,000-point bonus, scorpions are a juicy target. Unfortunately, they're hard to bring down. Crossing the screen on a straight line from left to right, most scorpions follow a path that's so high it's beyond the range of your gun.

Scorpions are troublesome. As each crosses the screen, it poisons every mushroom it touches. When a centipede comes in contact with a poisonous mushroom, it begins acting strangely, rushing headlong to the bottom of the screen, abandoning its usual zigzag movement.

When this occurs, you've got to move fast or you'll be wiped out. Position your gun so that the centipede falls directly toward it, and hold the fire button down for rapid-fire. If you shoot its head first, the centipede will regain its senses and resume its normal side-to-side manner of descent.

- The arrival of each spider, flea, or scorpion is signaled by a distinctive sound effect. Your ears are thus likely to know of the appearance of one of your enemies before your eyes.

- When all the centipedes have reached the bottom of the player's zone, one new head makes its appearance every five seconds at one of the upper corners of the zone. The heads continue to appear at a faster and faster rate—every three seconds, then every two seconds, and finally at the rate of one a second. Fleas, spiders, and scorpions are also entering the fray. You'll wish you had four pairs of eyes, six hands, and one gun for each hand. The end is near.

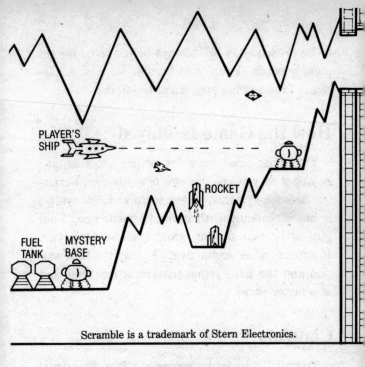

PLAYER'S SHIP

ROCKET

FUEL TANK

MYSTERY BASE

Scramble is a trademark of Stern Electronics.

SCRAMBLE

Scramble is not only exciting to play, it's a great game to watch. A jet plane sweeps over fast-changing landscapes, bombing and lasering enemy targets, dodging rockets, fireballs, and UFOs. There's more action in Scramble than in many a TV adventure show.

But after you've played Scramble a few times, you'll notice that the patterns repeat themselves. And therein lies the secret for mastering the game. If you memorize how the obstacles are arranged and can keep track of when they are going to be presented, you'll always be prepared for the game's perils. You'll also be able to take advantage of the scoring opportunities offered.

How the Game Is Played

You must pilot your jet plane, shooting and bombing as you go, through five different Scramble defense systems, called sectors. Each system is more challenging than the previous one. Your goal is the base station, which must be destroyed. It appears after sector five. Destroy the base station and the five-system pattern is repeated, but at a faster pace.

Controls

You pilot your jet by means of a four-directional joystick. Move the joystick to the right, and you speed up the plane. Moving it to the left slows the plane's speed. You cannot stop the plane or send it into reverse. Like a salmon swimming upstream, the jet never stops moving forward. You can also use the joystick to move the plane up and down.

You have a pushbutton to control your laser, which fires in bursts of four. A second pushbutton launches your bombs. Only two bombs can be in the air at the same time.

The laser always fires straight ahead, while the bombs fall to the earth in a gentle arc.

Scoring

When you destroy a UFO, you earn 100 points; destroying a mystery base earns 100, 200, or 300 points. Destroying the base station after sector five gets you 800 points. You also receive 10 points for every second your jet stays aloft.

Destroy a rocket on the ground and you receive 50 points. Destroying an airborne rocket is worth 80 points.

When you bomb a fuel tank, you gain 150 points. A fuel tank, when hit, also gets your jet a fuel bonus. This is important because your jet will crash should you let it run out of fuel.

You're given three jets at the beginning of a round. Whenever a jet is destroyed, the next one appears with fully loaded fuel tanks. If you accumulate 10,000 points, you earn a bonus jet.

Strategy and Tactics

- Your fuel supply is monitored by a timer that reports the amount of fuel remaining in terms of seconds. You must keep track of the timer's readings. When time begins to run out, concentrate on speed, that is, on completing the sector as fast as you can. Also concentrate on destroying fuel tanks. Forget about everything else.

- Here's a rundown on the strategy to use for each sector:

Sector One You fly over hills, valleys, and plateaus that are bristling with fuel tanks, mystery bases, and rockets. The best strategy is to fly almost at ground level, demolishing the targets with your laser. As you reach the top of each mountain, release a couple of bombs. They'll arc down into the valley beyond, destroying fuel tanks or mystery bases.

Move at a brisk speed. Keep an eye on your fuel supply. The only time to slow down is when targets appear in thick clusters, giving you a chance to swell your score.

The fuel tanks and mystery bases will not cause you any trouble. However, the rockets launched toward your ship are something of a problem. Slow down, let them leave the ground, and then blast them with your laser. Not only are the rockets easier to destroy once they are in the air, they're also worth more points.

Sector Two UFOs threaten you in this sector. They are unarmed, but colliding with one of them can mean death. Fly a straight path. Keep tapping both the laser and bomb buttons. You'll be able to destroy some of the UFOs on the ground. Those that manage to get into the air, pick off with your laser. You won't get them all, however. Some you'll have to dodge by up-and-down maneuvering. Others you'll simply have to outrace.

Sector Three Swarms of big fireballs are what

you have to avoid in this sector. Neither your bombs nor lasers are capable of destroying them. The valleys are places of safety. Flit down into a valley, let the fireballs stream by, and then rush over the mountain into the next valley.

As you zoom into a valley, destroy its mystery base and fuel tanks. Because of the time you spend taking shelter in the valleys, fuel— or lack of it—becomes a problem. Try to nail as many fuel tanks as you can during this sector.

Sector Four You're now flying over a big city. Towering skyscrapers and smaller structures make up the landscape. At times you must maneuver between tall buildings. Your steering skill is put to a severe test.

It's best to fly at medium speed. Not only are you less likely to collide with a skyscraper, but you'll have more time to laser and bomb the rockets and fuel tanks you'll see nestled on rooftops.

The city also contains dangerous rockets in deep silos. The silos are so deep, in fact, that your bombs have no effect on them. When approaching a rocket, turn on the speed. It's your best defense.

When you fly over a low roof that offers an assortment of inviting targets, swoop down low, just as if it were a wilderness valley, and laser everything in your path. But keep alert for the tall buildings that are going to suddenly loom up. You'll have to climb fast to avoid them.

Sector Five Now you're flying through a series of long and narrow brick tunnels. There's scarcely enough room for your jet.

The tunnels connect huge vertical caverns. Sometimes you will enter a cavern at one level and be forced to make your exit into the next tunnel at a different level. This means you have to exert very careful control of your ship. The slightest slip and you'll pile into a cavern wall.

As soon as you emerge from the tunnel into the cavern, slow down. Adjust the altitude of your jet for the passageway on the other side of the cavern. Once you have your jet at the right level, it's full speed ahead. When you enter the next cavern, repeat the cycle.

There's another problem you'll face in this sector. From time to time, rows of fuel tanks will block the tunnel passageway. Wipe out the tanks with your laser or you'll be destroyed.

● After making your way through the five Scramble defense systems, you finally reach the enemy base, an octagon-shaped structure with flashing lights. You must destroy the base. Your heart may sink the first time you see it. It lies at the bottom of a narrow canyon, so steep-walled that your bombs and laser seem of no value.

While you're trying to figure out what to do, you're using up fuel. What's the solution? Sacrifice your jet.

Thread your way into the canyon, pull up sharply, then release a bomb or fire your laser. Your aircraft will slam into one of the canyon walls. That's okay. You'll get a new ship at the start of the next round.

Many players, in an effort to avoid crashing, fly too high, and their bombs never reach the base. They don't realize that once the base has been destroyed, the jet has no further value.

- Once you've destroyed the base, another round begins. The same pattern is repeated, except that during each sector your fuel supply gets used up at a faster rate. Go for those fuel tanks.

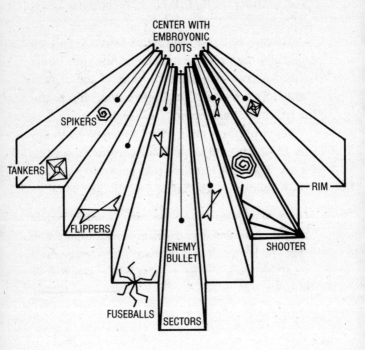

TEMPEST

A tempest, says the dictionary, is a violent disturbance. In this game, the violent disturbances are on the screen. They are all geometric designs formed out of wedge-shaped sections, each one alive with color and movement. Tempest is almost as exciting to watch as it is to play.

How the Game Is Played

Your weapon is a yellow diamond-shaped blaster that you move about the outside edge of the various playfields or sectors. Fierce aliens of various shapes and colors threaten to crash into the blaster and destroy it, and some of them have the ability to shoot it down. The aliens grow out of tiny dots that appear at the center of the board. They keep getting bigger and bigger as they make their way to the outer rim of the playfield. To stay alive, you must dodge the alien craft or blast them into nothingness.

Tempest offers 16 different boards, each a different pattern. After board 16, the sequence of patterns is repeated and the level of difficulty is increased. There are more aliens, and they move faster. The board numbers continue to go higher, all the way to board No. 99.

Controls

The control system is not difficult to master. On the right side of the console is a control knob that works like the knob on a radio, except that it is more sensitive, requiring a light touch. You spin it in either a clockwise or counterclockwise direction to move your blaster about the playfield's rim.

Your left hand controls a fire button. Hold the fire button down and you achieve rapid-fire, or almost rapid-fire, at any rate. A maximum of eight shots can be on the screen at one time.

Also on the left side of the screen is a super-zapper button. It can be used only once during each board. Press it and you destroy every alien on the screen.

Use the middle finger of your left hand to control the fire button. Use your left thumb to press the super-zapper button. You should be able to fire either button without looking down.

Scoring

A unique feature of Tempest is that it offers you a skill-level selection mode. You decide how difficult you want the game to be. You can start at skill-level one, three, five, seven, or nine. The game's control knob permits you to make the selection. You lock in your choice by pressing the fire button. When you've completed the board you've selected, you're rewarded as follows:

Board Number	Bonus Points
1	none
3	6,000
5	16,000
7	32,000
9	54,000

At the beginning of each game, you're given three blasters. You get a bonus blaster every time you accumulate 20,000 points. These figures can vary, however, depending on how the machine has been set.

There are five different enemy aliens. Each is a particular color; each has its own playing characteristics. Their point values are as follows:

Flippers Worth 150 points apiece, these creatures vault end over end as they move toward the outer edge of the playfield. Then they start flipping toward you, attempting to destroy the blaster. Beginners have more trouble with flippers than any of the other creatures.

Spikers First appearing on board three, spikers are worth 50 points. They create green lines as they move from the center of the board toward the blaster. These lines, called spikes, explode at the end of most boards. If the blaster is struck by an exploding spike, it is destroyed.

Tankers These creatures also first appear at board three. They're worth 100 points apiece. When hit, a tanker divides into two flippers. If not hit before it reaches the rim of the playfield, it breaks into flippers anyway.

Fuseballs You don't have to worry about fuseballs until board eleven. They drift along the lines that form the sectors. You can kill a fuseball by shooting it as it crosses between sector lines. Fuseballs are worth 250, 500, or 700 points.

Pulsars First appearing on board 17, pulsars cause sectors of the board to flash white. If the blaster happens to enter a sector that is pulsing, it is destroyed. You can shoot a pulsar when it is not pulsing. You get 200 points.

Strategy and Tactics

- Learn to identify the various aliens by their colors. They vary as follows:

Board No.	Flipper	Tanker	Spiker	Pulsar
1–16	Orange	Purple	Green	—
17–32	Purple	Blue	Light blue	Yellow
33–48	Green	Blue	Green	Purple

Fuseballs are always multicolored.

- As soon as the screen lights up, start firing. Simply fire blindly toward the center of the board. The aliens will just be emerging from the tiny dots, and you'll manage to destroy some of them. This will make your life easier in the later stages of the game.

- The first two boards, in which you compete only against flippers, should not cause you great difficulty. As the flippers emerge from the center of the playfield, fire away at them. Don't limit your fire to the particular sector in which a flipper happens to be located. Spread your fire over three or four sectors. This makes missing much more unlikely.

- If a flipper reaches the playfield's outer rim, you still don't have to be concerned. You always have your super-zapper, which can destroy every flipper on the board, although others may rise from the center.

- If you have used your super-zapper and more flippers threaten you, select one sector as your base sector. Pick out one at either the extreme right or left of the playfield. Then start firing as rapidly as you can. This means tapping the fire button at a mad pace. As each flipper nears your blaster, it will be chopped down. This holds true even if two flippers approach from opposite directions.

- The third board is more troublesome. Two new enemies appear: tankers and spikers. When you shoot a tanker, it becomes two flippers, and then they must be destroyed.

  Go after the tankers and the flippers they form, spraying your shots over several sectors. Concentrate on the tankers and flippers that are closest to the rim. Fire continuously.

  Spikers are a less serious threat. By firing at them, you whittle them down in size and eventually destroy them.

  Spikers create lines that can destroy you. The message AVOID SPIKERS appears on the screen at the end of the board. Move the blaster into a sector where no spikers are located. Fail to do so and you will be destroyed by an exploding spiker.

- On level nine, spikers occupy every level of the playfield. You must be certain that you clear at least one sector of spikers, and then take refuge in that sector before the board ends.

Again, select one sector as your base sector, one on the extreme right or left of the playfield. Clear that sector of all spikers. Blast away at those other aliens in those sectors closest to your base. Ignore the other sectors.

- At level eleven, fuseballs make their first appearance. They move up and down the various sectors of the playfield, following no particular pattern. Fuseballs can be destroyed only when they are moving from one sector to another.

  When a fuseball reaches the outer rim of the playfield, it is a great hazard. The slightest contact with one will destroy your blaster. If you have already used your super-zapper, try waiting out the fuseball. Clear an escape route for yourself by destroying flippers. The fuseballs move very slowly. The game is likely to have advanced to the next level before the fuseball reaches you.

- At level seventeen, you're confronted with pulsars for the first time. Pulsars flip from place to place in much the same way flippers do. After flipping, a pulsar will stop in one of the sectors and start to pulse. This causes the borders of the sector to flash white. Should you enter a sector that is occupied by a flashing pulsar, you will be destroyed.

  The time to shoot a pulsar is when it is moving from one sector to the next. Wait for it to stop pulsing. It will then flip to the next sector. That's when to shoot it.

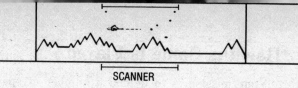

SCANNER

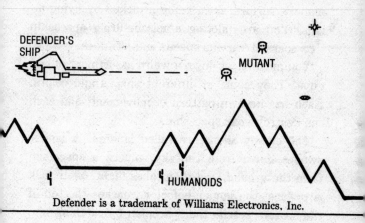

DEFENDER'S SHIP

MUTANT

HUMANOIDS

Defender is a trademark of Williams Electronics, Inc.

DEFENDER

If you're a beginner, stay away from Defender. It will gulp down your quarters faster than a Las Vegas slot machine. You can, however, learn to master the machine if you practice constantly, achieving scores of from 50,000 to 100,000. Fifteen-year-old Steve Juraszek, a world record-holder in Defender, started playing the game one June day not long ago. He played every day without missing. By the time vacation was over and school bells were ringing again, Steve had his record. His mother said: "I just wish he was that good about doing his homework."

How the Game Is Played

Your mission is to defend a number of spacemen, sprinkled at various intervals along the planet's surface, from being attacked by flying aliens. You are piloting a missile-firing spaceship that soars at various speeds and altitudes.

You must shoot down a weird assortment of bad guys. They come in different shapes and colors. Each has its own pattern of movement, and each can destroy your spaceship.

The enemy aliens are called landers. A lander swoops down from the sky, plucks a spaceman from the ground, and then takes flight. Your task is to blast the lander before it reaches the top of the screen, rescue the spaceman by catching him in midair, and return him safely to the ground.

You're given ten spacemen at the beginning of each wave or round. If the aliens should kidnap all ten of them, or they are otherwise destroyed, your planet disappears. You then find yourself in outer space facing the bad guys. Your end is near.

If, on the other hand, you're successful in fighting off the waves of attackers, you're rewarded with a new set of spacemen and a new planet. Everything begins anew at a slightly faster pace.

Controls

It's not hard to understand the plot of Defender. It's you and your spaceship against all those bad guys. What causes the problems is the control system. There are more controls in this game than in any other. You must learn to manipulate them skillfully to score even a few thousand points.

You control a joystick that determines your spaceship's altitude, moving it up or down; and there are five separate buttons that fire your missiles, change forward thrust, reverse your ship's direction, send the ship into hyperspace, and fire your smart bombs, which blow up everything in sight.

It's not quite as difficult as it may sound. The fingers of your left hand are on the joystick, controlling the vertical movement of your ship. The reverse button, which changes the heading of your ship, is just beneath your left thumb.

Your right hand controls the fire button and the thrust button. The fire button, which launches your missiles, is not automatic; it's semiautomatic. You must tap-and-release, tap-and-release. The thrust button sends the ship through space. You'll be pushing almost continuously.

That leaves just two more buttons: the hyperspace button and the smart-bomb button. You use them only occasionally. (Some players *never* press hyperspace.) The hyperspace button, located in the very center of the control board, causes your ship to vanish and then reappear at some random location on the screen.

The smart-bomb button, a green button, is located just below the thrust button. It's your problem-solver. When pressed, it destroys all the aliens on the screen. What could be better than that? When the game starts you have three smart bombs.

As a beginner, don't be concerned about the reverse or hyperspace buttons. Concentrate on using the thrust button and fire button together (with the fingers of the right hand), while you control the ship's altitude with the joystick (and the fingers of your left hand). Go easy on the thrust button, however. If you use too much thrust, you'll lose control of your ship and be quickly wiped out.

Scoring

Landers are the first of the enemies that you face. A lander drifts out of the atmosphere to the planet floor, seeking to capture a spaceman. When successful, it attempts to carry the captive to the top of the screen. There the spaceman and the lander merge to form another enemy, a mutant. Both the landers and the mutants fire white bombs at your spaceship.

You earn 150 points whenever you destroy a lander or a mutant. When you catch a spaceman in midair after destroying a mutant, you earn a bonus of 500 points. When you safely deposit a spaceman on the planet surface, you earn another 500 points. When a spaceman lands by himself on the planet after you've destroyed a lander, you get 250 points.

Baiters, which look like clusters of short dashes, are another enemy you face on the first screen. The longer it takes you to complete the round, the more baiters appear. They also fire white bombs. Destroying a baiter is worth 200 points.

Bombers, pods, and swarmers make their appearance in the second round. Bombers are small square boxes. When they come close to your spaceship they drop off tiny X's, which can destroy you. You get 250 points for destroying a bomber. Pods take the form of purple and blue stars. Each is worth 1,000 points. When you destroy a pod, groups of swarmers appear. Destroying a swarmer is worth 150 points.

You're also given bonus points whenever you complete a round. This bonus is calculated by multiplying the number of spacemen you have remaining by 100 for round one, by 200 for round two, by 300 for round three, 400 for round four, and 500 for all the rounds that follow.

Last, you're given a bonus spaceship and a smart bomb for every 10,000 points you score.

Strategy and Tactics

- As the first round begins, concentrate on zapping landers. If you're successful in destroying them quickly, you won't have to worry about mutants and baiters.

  Try to keep your spaceship at about ground level, dodging mountaintops when necessary.

That's where most of the landers prefer to fly.

- While it's possible for you to drop below the planet's surface, do so only when you're fleeing attackers. You're away from the landers at that level. You also run the risk of wiping out one of your spacemen with a stray missile.

- Keep tapping the fire button, sending out missiles as fast as you can. There's no limit to the number of missiles in your arsenal and no penalty for missing shots.

- At the top of the screen is a radar scanner. It shows a much broader view of the planet, but in miniature. All of your enemies can be seen on the scanner, so you instantly become aware of where you are needed the most. As you become more experienced, learn to use the scanner and the information it provides. It's like catching a glimpse of the future. It's vital to achieving really high scores.

- Conserve your smart bombs. You'll need them in the later rounds when you'll be confronted with a greater number of enemies traveling at faster speeds.

- Hyperspace should be used only in emergencies. When you press hyperspace, you run the risk of destroying your spaceship when it reappears in the screen.

Chapter 4

ALL ABOUT PAC-MAN (AND MS. PAC-MAN)

There are no enemy aliens, no evil robots. It's a game that has nothing to do with war, shooting, or outer space. There are no fire buttons, warp buttons, or hyperspace buttons. Yet it is the most successful of all video games. It's Pac-Man, of course, the first video game hit of the 1980s.

Pac-Man packs arcades and other sites where it is found. Kids line up to play it. Home versions of the game are available from Atari and Coleco and many other firms.

Pac-Man products seem to be everywhere. You can wear a Pac-Man T-shirt or Pac-Man pajamas. You can put Pac-Man laces in your shoes. You can send Pac-Man greeting cards to your friends and wrap their gifts in Pac-Man wrapping paper. You can tell time by a Pac-Man clock or wristwatch. You can drink from a Pac-Man mug. "Pac-Man Fe-

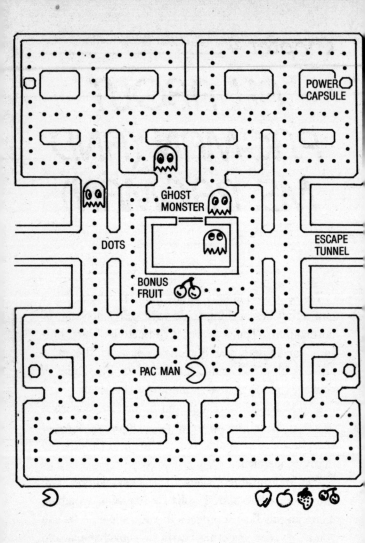

POWER
CAPSULE

GHOST
MONSTER

DOTS

ESCAPE
TUNNEL

BONUS
FRUIT

PAC MAN

Pac-Man is a trademark of Midway Manufacturing Company.

ver" resounds from countless radios and record players. And, naturally, there are Pac-Man bumper stickers.

No one knows for sure how many Pac-Man machines are out there in arcadeland. Some sources say the number is 200,000. Other sources say the number may be twice that. One thing is certain: Pac-Man is the most popular arcade game in history.

Every few years America is struck by a fad. There was the Hula-Hoop and Davy Crockett. There were pop rocks and pet rocks. Now there is Pac-Man, a craze that threatens to outdo all the others.

PAC-MAN

How the Game Is Played

Pac-Man has a very simple theme. The yellow disc that is Pac-Man gobbles up small gold dots and an occasional piece of fruit while four fuzzy monsters try to gobble him up.

When Pac-Man is devoured by a monster, he withers away like a delicate flower in the hot sun. You're given three Pac-Men at the beginning of each game.

All of this unfolds within the borders of a maze. You control a joystick that moves Pac-Man through the corriders of the maze—left or right, up or down.

The maze passageways are lined with 240 small gold dots. There are larger dots, called energizers or power capsules, in each corner of the maze. These energizers are important. When Pac-Man eats one, the monsters turn dark blue in color and can then be eaten by Pac-Man.

When the monsters are about to change back from dark blue to their original colors, they flash blue and white. Take this as a warning. If you're pursuing a monster and he begins blinking, give up the chase. By the time you catch him, he's likely to be his original color again and capable of eating you.

At each side of the maze, there's an entrance to a tunnel. It also serves as the tunnel exit. Pac-Man and the monsters have the ability to enter the tunnel at one side of the screen, disappear briefly, and reenter the board on the opposite side.

Even though Pac-Man may be in the tunnel and out of sight, he is not safe. The monsters are capable of eating Pac-Man when he is in the tunnel and not visible, but he is also capable of eating dark blue monsters during this period.

If you're successful in clearing the board of all 240 dots and the four energizers, another board appears, and the game begins anew. Each board is identified by a symbol, usually a piece of fruit.

With each board you complete, the game gets more difficult. Pac-Man and the monsters travel at faster speeds. You're forced to make decisions quicker. The chance of making a fatal mistake thus increases.

In still later boards, the monsters move at an even faster pace, while Pac-Man's speed is slower. Also, as the boards change, the length of time the monsters remain blue (and can be eaten by Pac-Man) gets shorter and shorter. In the first three or four boards, the monsters remain blue for six or seven seconds. But in later boards, the time span is only two or three seconds. And toward the end of the board sequence, the monsters do not turn blue at all. In such cases, don't even bother to chase them. You have to play defensively.

There may come a time when you feel quite adept at the game. Your difficulties aren't over, however. The more skilled you become, the longer you're able to play. The longer you play, the fewer quarters the arcade gets.

When this starts happening, the arcade owner is likely to reset the game so everything is speeded up. Or a new microprocessor will be inserted, changing the game's program. Tactics that once enabled you to score 25,000 or so will now lead to sudden death. You'll have to relearn the machine. (Well, there's always stamp collecting.)

Controls

You maneuver Pac-Man with a four-position joystick, the game's only control system. Strive for a light touch with the joystick. If you grip tightly, you'll never be able to move Pac-Man with the ease and smoothness necessary for high scores.

Scoring

There are several ways to score points. Each time Pac-Man eats a dot, you get 10 points. Each time Pac-Man devours an energizer, you get 50 points.

You also earn points for gobbling up the dark blue monsters. The first blue monster eaten earns 200 points; the second, 400 points; the third, 800 points; and the fourth, 1,600 points. Thus, if you're able to eat all four of the monsters you add a total of 3,000 points to your score (1,600 + 800 + 400 + 200 = 3,000).

It's no cinch to do this, however. For the short period the monsters are blue, they're very shifty, darting every which way to escape you.

As mentioned above, when Pac-Man has eaten all the dots and energizers, another screen appears. Each screen in the sequence is identified by a symbol, which is usually a fruit. You get points for eating these symbols, which appear just below the maze's center box. The point values for the symbols are as follows:

Board Number	Symbol	Point Value
1	Cherries	100
2	Strawberry	300
3	1st Orange (or Peach)	500
4	2nd Orange (or Peach)	500
5	1st Apple	700
6	2nd Apple	700
7	1st Pineapple (or Grape)	1,000
8	2nd Pineapple (or Grape)	1,000
9	1st Galaxian	2,000
10	2nd Galaxian	2,000
11	1st Bell	3,000
12	2nd Bell	3,000
13	1st Key	5,000
14	2nd Key	5,000
15	3rd Key	5,000
16, etc.	Keys	5,000

The fruit or other symbol also appears in the lower right-hand corner of the screen, just below the maze border, This appearance of the fruit is simply to identify which screen is being played. Since it's actually off the board, there's no chance it can be eaten by Pac-Man.

If you should reach a score of 10,000, you get a bonus Pac-Man. (On some machines, you must get 15,000 points before the extra Pac-Man is awarded.) You never get more than one bonus Pac-Man, no matter how high a score you achieve.

Strategy and Tactics

Do you remember the first time you put a quarter into a Pac-Man machine? Before you realized what was happening, the four monsters were chasing you. Frantically working the joystick, you moved Pac-Man left and right, up and down, munching as many dots as possible. You gasped when Pac-Man collided with a monster, was quickly eaten, and disappeared from the screen.

A second Pac-Man appeared, and then a third, and both met the same fate.

The game lasted about one minute. You chalked up a score of 600 or 700, or, if you were lucky, perhaps 1,400 or 1,500.

You then probably did what most players do— put another quarter into the machine, and another and another and another.

Little by little, your scores got better. Maybe you got so you could score as many as 4,000 or 5,000 points per quarter.

That's fine, but you should be able to do much better than that. Evidence of this is the day's high scores, which are posted at the top of the screen. Check them toward the end of a busy day in the arcade. You'll see numbers like 68,100 and 109,400, and maybe even 238,700.

You can rack up scores of this type. Maybe you can even become a Pac-Master, a player who consistently scores 150,000 or higher.

There are two ways to improve in Pac-Man. One is to learn certain offensive and defensive tactics, and then use them every time you play. The other method is to memorize carefully mapped-out patterns that enable Pac-Man to outwit the monsters, and use these patterns over and over again.

The pages that follow instruct in both of these methods:

- At the beginning of a board, immediately start devouring dots. Save the energizers for last. Try to wait until at least three monsters are nearby before you eat an energizer. This gives you a chance to devour the monsters, which builds your score.

- The areas of greatest danger are the four corners of the board and the long horizontal pathway at the bottom. This is because the monsters can enter these areas from more than one direction, entrapping you. Avoid these areas whenever possible.

- The safest areas are the pathways surrounding the center box. There is also an area of safety within the two S-shaped pathways just above the center box. (The pathway on the left is actually a reverse S.) The monsters will never enter the S passages from below, only from above. A skilled player can lead the monsters around the S pathways and the area surrounding the center box for long periods of time without being caught.

- Watch a veteran player and you'll notice how he gets Pac-Man to rush around the screen without ever breaking stride. There's never a moment's hesitation before a turn. The only time Pac-Man stops is when the player wants him to stop.

The secret of getting Pac-Man to whiz along is to signal him to turn before he gets to the turn. Suppose Pac-Man is hurrying along and you want him to make a left turn. Move the joystick to the left just before Pac-Man gets to the turn. He'll make the turn without a moment's delay.

- Pac-Man travels fastest in a pathway without dots. Thus when monsters are in close pursuit, you have a better chance of outrunning them if you take a dotless path.

- It's important to understand the personality of each of the monsters. By so doing, you'll often be able to predict what each is going to do.

The red monster is named Shadow. It's a name that is well chosen, because Shadow is usually trailing after Pac-Man, sometimes practically snapping at his heels. This isn't as serious as it sounds, for Pac-Man can outrun Shadow, particularly if Pac-Man keeps turning corners. Shadow is lead-footed when making a turn, as are the other monsters.

The pink monster, named Speedy, can outrace Pac-Man (unless Pac-Man turns corners at a rapid clip). Speedy, in fact, is the only monster who is faster than Pac-Man.

Speedy likes to enter the tunnel from the left side. Don't enter from the right side if a monster is trailing you and Speedy is near the tunnel entrance on the other side. You're likely to be committing suicide.

The light blue monster is very shy. Bashful is his name. He is so shy that if you make a threatening move toward him, Bashful will often veer away, turning into an intersection if one happens to be available.

Bashful has the habit of entering the tunnel at random times during a game. Once he's within the tunnel and not visible, Bashful loses his shyness. If you enter the tunnel from the opposite side, Bashful may gobble you up. Never enter the tunnel if Bashful is entering at the other side or is anywhere near the entrance.

The orange monster, Pokey, is not a big threat. He's slow afoot; you can always outrun him. In addition, Pokey gets a bit confused at times, forgetting his mission. For example, sometimes when Pokey is chasing Pac-Man and Pac-Man makes a turn, Pokey will keep going straight ahead. Maybe the poor guy just needs a rest.

Each of the monsters has a corner of the screen that he favors. Shadow, who is always the first one out of the center box at the beginning of the game, prefers the upper right corner of the board. Bashful, the second monster out of the box, heads for the upper left corner. Pokey calls the lower left corner home. Speedy favors the lower right corner.

At random times during the game, the monsters suddenly stop chasing Pac-Man and head for their respective corners. But don't worry, they'll be back.

THE MONSTERS

Color	Name	Nickname	Leading Trait	Favorite Corner
Red	Shadow	Blinky	Pursuing	Upper right
Pink	Speedy	Pinky	Speed	Lower right
Light blue	Bashful	Inky	Shyness	Upper left
Orange	Pokey	Clyde	Slowness	Lower left

• Learn to watch the monsters' eyes, not the monsters as a whole. The eyes roll to face in the direction the monsters plan to travel.

• Being bold sometimes pays rich dividends. When you are being pursued, try making an abrupt 180-degree change of direction. In other words, you end up facing your pursuer. This sometimes causes the monster to veer to the right or left. Don't try such tactics, however, when racing down a long straightaway. There has to be an intersection between you and the monster, someplace for him to turn into.

• Learn to use the tunnel to outwit the monsters. Remember, you pick up speed as you enter the tunnel, and thus you can usually outrace them on the trip from one end to the other.

When you enter the tunnel and one or more monsters continue to pursue you, quickly reverse direction, and then reverse direction again, resuming your original course. By pretending to head toward your pursuers, you can make them slow down. At other times, this tactic will cause the monsters to change course and head off in some other direction and not enter the tunnel at all.

- When monsters are on your trail, don't make any turns. The monsters react immediately when you do this and will take a shortcut and nab you.

- Try to devour the fruit or other prize whenever it appears on the screen. Doing so gives your score a big boost.

- If you are trapped between two monsters, each advancing toward you, you have no hope—unless one of them is looking away from you. In such a case, you'll be able to follow that monster to safety.

- When only one energizer and a few dots remain in one corner of the screen, do not eat them right away. Wait until the monsters are close. Otherwise, you won't be able to catch any of the monsters when they turn blue.

Pattern Play

Having Pac-Man follow certain carefully mapped-out pathways through the maze is a near-perfect way of gaining mastery over this game. One such pattern is offered in this section. It applies to the first screen, the one that displays a pair of cherries. Follow the pattern and you'll consume all the dots and energizers; the next screen will then be presented to you.

Practice is vital if you expect to become successful at using patterns. You must memorize the pattern and be able to direct Pac-Man through it without the slightest hesitation.

You'll be able to memorize a pattern quickly if you sketch it a few times. Make some photo copies of the diagram of the Pac-Man maze that appears on page 114. Draw the pattern on one of the copies. As you draw, try to commit the pattern to memory.

Test whether you've memorized the pattern by attempting to draw it without referring to the book. You should memorize the pattern so well that you're able to draw it in the blink of an eye.

Keep in mind that you have to memorize the pattern *perfectly*. The slightest variation can render the pattern worthless.

Pac-Man must move smoothly through the pattern. There can't be the slightest delay at any point. When Pac-Man hesitates, the monsters react to the hesitation. They're then likely to

Chart A

move in a direction that the pattern does not allow
for. And that movement can be fatal to Pac-Man.

As Chart A shows, much of the lower portion of
the board is cleared of dots in the opening stages
of the pattern. You then enter the tunnel on the

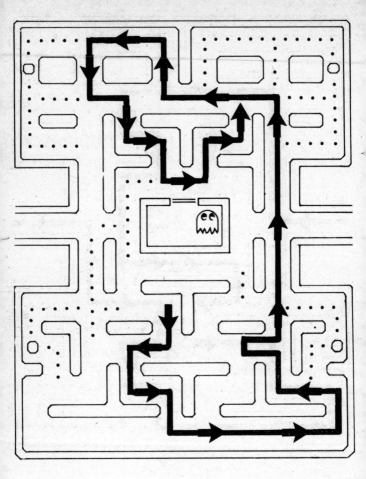

Chart B

right side, reappear on the left side, head north, cut across the board, and then circle around the box from the right side to eat the fruit.

In Chart B you continue finishing off the horizontal row of dots at the bottom of the screen and

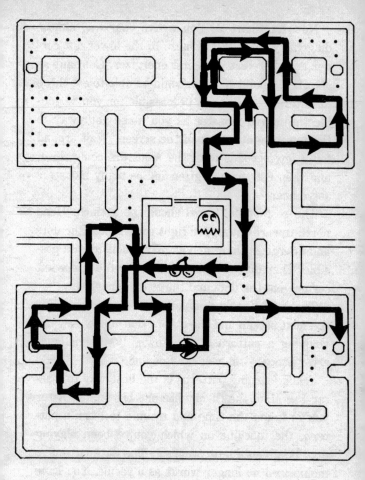

Chart C

clearing the long vertical row as you race to the top of the board. You make a U-turn near the upper left corner of the screen. A monster seems ready to pounce upon you at this point. Don't worry; nothing will happen. Continue as shown.

Now for Chart C. You weave your way almost diagonally through the maze to the lower left corner and there eat your first energizer. Continue as shown. At point X, you should be able to eat three monsters. It may even be possible for you to gobble the fourth monster as you make your way to the lower right corner of the screen. Wait around for a few seconds until the monsters come close, and then eat the energizer and as many monsters as you can.

The rest of the board should be a cinch. Head north toward the upper right corner. Eat the dots and energizer there and as many monsters as possible. Then dart across the screen to the upper left corner, eat the dots and the fourth energizer.

That's it! You've completed the first screen. For the next screen and the others that follow, try developing a pattern of your own. It's a trial-and-error process—as you can imagine.

While learning patterns is the best way to master Pac-Man, the theory has one big failing. After you've taken the time and trouble to learn a pattern, the machine on which you've been playing may be given a new program. The pattern you've memorized no longer works as a result. You have to develop a new pattern or find a machine that's identical to the one you've been playing.

MS. PAC-MAN

The success of Space Invaders led to Space Invaders II. Because Asteroids was such a big hit, we have Asteroids Deluxe. The same thing was bound to happen to Pac-Man. Late in 1981, at the crest of the game's popularity, the Midway Company shut down the Pac-Man production line and began switching over to the game's successor, Ms. Pac-Man. The new game began showing up in arcades across the country early in 1982.

If you're a Pac-Man fan, the Ms. Pac-Man will look very familiar to you. There are the same brightly colored monsters pursuing the yellow disc. The disc gobbles up dots and, by eating an energizer, can turn the table on the monsters and start devouring them.

The disc has changed, however. It wears a tiny red ribbon at the top of its head, there's a dab of lipstick at its mouth, and it has long, curly eyelashes. Oh, yes, during one of the halftime shows that occur between screens, Baby Pac-Man makes an appearance. Perhaps there's a Baby Pac-Man game in the future.

There are several differences in the two games. The most important difference has to do with the mazes. In the original Pac-Man, there is only one maze. But in Ms. Pac-Man, there are three different mazes. Each has a distinctive color. For this reason, pattern play doesn't work (unless the pattern you're using happens to apply to the particular maze you're playing).

In two of the game's three different mazes, two tunnels are offered. This gives you a much greater opportunity to escape monsters who are in close pursuit.

Here's a rundown on the boards:

Board Number	Maze Color	Symbol	Point Value
1	Salmon	Cherries	100
2	Salmon	Strawberry	200
3	Blue	Orange	500
4	Blue	Pretzel	700
5	Blue	Apple	1,000
6	Orange	Pear	2,000
7	Orange	Banana	5,000
8	?	?	100 to 5,000

In board eight and the boards that follow, any one of the seven symbols can appear. You receive the point value that normally applies to that symbol.

Strategy and Tactics

The basic methods of play you use in Pac-Man should also be put to use in Ms. Pac-Man. Devour the dots as quickly as you can. Save the energizers for last. You can outmaneuver the monsters by making a series of quick turns or using the tunnels.

Each of the mazes demands different tactics. When playing the salmon board, notice that there's a big square of dots at the center. Moving in a counterclockwise direction from the starting box, clear that entire square. Take evasive action if a monster challenges you, but then return to devouring the dots. When you've finished with the square, clear the dots that appear between the bottom edge of the square and the bottom of the screen.

The blue maze is a bit more difficult. Although it offers two tunnels, one of them is at the very top of the board and is not easy to reach. If you have problems with this board, it is likely to be in the upper regions of it. Clear the dots from the lower regions first. As you do, be sure to leave yourself avenues of approach to the upper regions.

The monsters move faster and stay blue for shorter periods in the orange board. Again, there are two tunnels. Both are easy to reach. This board shouldn't cause you any great difficulty.

OTHER PAC-MEN

Pac-Man is not only available as a coin-operated arcade game. Atari has been licensed to distribute a Pac-Man cartridge for use with the company's Video Computer System. The Coleco Company produces a battery-powered, table-model Pac-Man.

There are also illegal imitations of Pac-Man. They are almost identical to the original game, but they have different names. One is called Puck-

Man. Another goes by the name of Munch-Man.

Finally, there are several Pac-Man cousins. These are arcade games that feature bright colors, a maze, a catchy melody, and a charming little character that races around in the screen, his life threatened by devious enemies of one type or another. You may have seen some of these games. They include Mouse Trap, Lock 'N' Chase, and Turtles.

Atari's Pac-Man

There are several differences between the arcade Pac-Man and the Atari home game. These differences affect how the game is played.

One of these differences is obvious at just a quick glance. In the Atari version, Pac-Man eats dashes, not dots. But the object of the game is the same: to earn the highest possible score by eating dashes and energizers, while avoiding being eaten by the monsters.

There's another difference you'll notice right away. Because the game is played on your home television set screen, the board is greater in width than it is in length. (Arcade game screens are greater in length than in width.)

The maze is different, too. Instead of 240 dots, you're presented with 126 dashes. And the tunnel, instead of extending from one side of the board to the other, runs from top to bottom.

The Atari version of Pac-Man himself isn't quite the same, either. He's still small and yellow and has a very big mouth, but the Atari people have given him a squarish shape and a tiny eye. All of the monsters are yellow in the Atari game, and they blink rapidly on and off during the game. Incidentally, Atari doesn't call them monsters, but refers to them as ghosts.

Besides consuming dots and energizers, Pac-Man, in the arcade version, also devours various symbols that appear just below the center box. These symbols identify the screen being played. They change from a pair of cherries to a strawberry, include several other fruits, and end in a series of keys. But Atari's symbol is a tiny gold rectangle, which the company calls a vitamin.

One thing that makes the Atari game easier is that you're given four Pac-Men, not three, at the beginning of a game. And you get an additional Pac-Man every time you complete a board.

How the Game Is Played

The Atari cartridge offers sixteen different versions of Pac-Man. Eight are solitaire games, and eight are two-player contests. The basics of the game do not change from one variation to the other, but the degree of difficulty does. In some, the ghosts blunder about the board, quickly falling prey to Pac-Man. Completing board after board is a cinch. It's great for your ego. But in other versions, Pac-Man and the ghosts zip about the board at an extremely fast pace, and the ghosts seemed to be guided by radar in their ability to seek out and home in on poor Pac-Man.

The Atari version of Pac-Man demands that you become a much more careful player, a more cautious player. The joystick is a case in point. In the arcade game, the joystick is a precision instrument. Pac-Man reacts instantly to its movement, carrying out your commands exactly. But in the home version, the joystick has a clumsy feel. It doesn't give you the precise response that you expect. Move it boldly or aggressively and you're likely to find yourself overshooting the mark. Eventually, you'll get the feel of the instrument, but at first it is likely to cause you some problems.

In the arcade version, all Pac-Man has to do is touch a dot and it disappears; he's eaten it. But with the Atari game, Pac-Man must completely overlap a dash in order to gobble it down. This variation takes some getting used to, too.

While it's more difficult for Pac-Man to swallow his prey, the monsters have it easier. In the arcade game, Pac-Man is involved in many a close call, and there are times when a monster may even partially overtake Pac-Man, but he escapes. That doesn't happen in the home game. The slightest contact between Pac-Man and a ghost means lights out for Pac-Man.

The Atari game operates a bit differently after Pac-Man has eaten an energizer. Recall what happens in the arcade game—the monsters turn dark blue, during which time they can be eaten by Pac-Man. Before they turn back to their original colors, they flash briefly between blue and white. The flashing is a signal that they're about to become dangerous again.

In the home version, the ghosts turn blue after Pac-Man has eaten an energizer, just as in the arcade game. But before they turn back to their original color of yellow, they change to pink. But because the ghosts are very pale and constantly flashing on and off, the change to pink can be difficult to notice. You're likely to get trapped a few times before you realize what's happening.

Atari may have realized this failing, for the cartridge provides a second signal to warn you that the ghosts are about to become dangerous again. It's an audio signal, not a visual one, taking the form of a high-pitched sound. It begins right after Pac-Man has eaten the energizer, and it stops abruptly just before the ghosts change back to yellow and become eaters again. So when you hear that high-pitched warning sound end, flee!

Some home players prefer the game in its black-and-white mode. This makes the color change more obvious, with the ghosts taking on distinctive tones of gray instead of adopting confusing pastel colors.

Be sure to reread the tips given earlier in this chapter. They apply to the Atari home game as well as to the arcade version. Overall, you can't be quite as bold when playing the home game. You have to think more defensively. You'll spend more time using the tunnel to elude or escape your pursuers. You'll spend more time in the safe areas of the board, that is, in the pathways surrounding the center box and the S-shaped pathways above it.

Coleco's Pac-Man

Coleco, a Hartford, Connecticut, toy manufacturer, offers a table-model version of Pac-Man that is compact, light in weight, and operates on four C batteries. But when you play Portable Pac-Man, as Coleco has named the game, don't expect the same excitement you get from the arcade game. It's not as challenging, either. It's something like riding a tricycle after tooling around for a while on a ten-speed racer.

Portable Pac-Man does give you variety, however. It offers not only a program that is similar to the one encountered in the arcades, but two other versions of it: Head-to-Head Pac-Man and Eat-and-Run. Both of these are described later in this chapter.

In the standard version of Portable Pac-Man, you're given three Pac-Men, just as in the coin-operated game. There are many fewer dots, only 64, as compared to 240 in the arcade version.

The scoring is a bit different. You earn 10 points for each dot eaten and 50 points for eating an energizer, but only 100, 200, 400, and 800 points for eating a monster after an energizer has been eaten. As you probably realize, these point values are one-half of those that you earn for eating arcade-game monsters. So if your score isn't quite up to your arcade standard, don't let it bother you.

The energizers are blinking red dots. After an energizer has been eaten by Pac-Man, and the monsters are subject to being eaten, they do not turn dark blue. Instead, their bodies disappear but their eyes remain. So Pac-Man doesn't actually eat entire monsters; he consumes only eyes.

When the monsters' bodies are about to return, the game emits a high-pitched sound. This is your warning that the monsters are about to become dangerous. Act accordingly—skip away.

There are no fruit symbols in Portable Pac-Man. Each board thus offers the same number of potential points.

The biggest difference in Portable Pac-Man and the arcade version is in the general layout of the board. Portable Pac-Man's board is much smaller and squarish in shape, and the maze is a good deal less complicated.

This means that the patterns of play common to the coin-operated game don't apply to Portable Pac-Man. And many of the playing tips you may have learned have little value.

Nevertheless, if you're skilled in the arcade version of Pac-Man, you should have no trouble excelling in Portable Pac-Man. Your basic knowledge of the game and your ability to call upon basic offensive and defensive tactics should be enough to make you a superior player.

HEAD-TO-HEAD PAC-MAN

This is a two-player game, with you and your opponent each handling a joystick that controls a Pac-Man. The idea is to outscore your opponent by eating as many dots, monsters, and energizers as possible. Both players' scores are posted continuously throughout the game.

Head-to-Head Pac-Man has a frantic quality to it. The two Pac-Men sometimes collide or their paths cross. Indeed, there may be times when you lose track of which Pac-Man is yours and which is your opponent's.

What's vital in playing Head-to-Head Pac-Man is that you keep alive for as long as you possibly can. Do everything in your power to avoid being eaten by a monster. Your hope, of course, is that your opponent will be eaten. Then you can continue to play, consuming dots, energizers, and monsters, building up your point total. You can, in fact, continue to play through board after board, burying your opponent in an avalanche of points.

While keeping alive should be your chief strategy, there are several other tactics you can pursue to increase your score. Suppose your opponent eats an energizer. Either of you can then begin to devour monsters. But it's not always wise to rush in and gobble down the first monster you encounter. Remember that the point values for eating monsters are 100 for the first monster, 200 for the second, 400 for the third, and 800 for the fourth. Your best strategy may be to delay slightly. Let your opponent capture the first monster, while you take the second. You'll then have outscored your opponent by 100 points. (Your opponent will have earned 100 points; you'll have earned 200.) Or let him consume the first and second monsters, while you eat the third. Again, you'll have earned 100 points more than he has earned. (He will have 300 points; you will have 400.)

The strategy of delaying also applies after *you've* eaten a monster. If your opponent wants to speed to the scene and grab off a monster as quickly as he can, let him. Remember, patience can earn higher point totals.

As you and your opponent duel, you're likely to find that Head-to-Head Pac-Man is even more challenging than the standard version, for you not only have to outmaneuver the monsters, but you have to outwit a human opponent as well.

EAT-AND-RUN PAC-MAN

This might be called "Reverse Pac-Man" because certain aspects of the game are just the opposite of what occurs in the standard version. The game begins with Pac-Man in the center box. The monsters are posted outside. When Pac-Man makes his exit, he darts about the board eating energizers (there are no dots) while the monsters pursue him. You must keep from being eaten and return to the safety of the center box. Every time you get back to the box safely, you've completed a "run."

If you fail to eat any energizers, the door to the box does not open. You get 100 points for the first energizer you eat, 200 points for the second energizer, 400 for the third, and 800 for the fourth. But if you fail to get back to the center box, no points are recorded, no matter how many energizers are eaten.

The points awarded for eating energizers increase dramatically after you've made four successful runs, as this chart shows:

	First Energizer	Second Energizer	Third Energizer	Fourth Energizer
First 4 runs	100	200	400	800
After 4 runs	200	400	800	1,600
After 8 runs	300	600	1,200	2,400
After 12 runs	400	800	1,600	3,200
After 16 runs	500	1,000	2,000	4,000

As this chart suggests, the key to building a high point total is completing the first four runs successfully. Eat just one energizer and return to the center box, thus completing a successful run. The points you can earn by eating a second, third, or fourth energizer aren't worth the risk of being devoured by the monsters. Follow this strategy until you've completed the first four runs. You'll then have the opportunity to try for the much higher point totals that apply in the game's later stages.

Chapter 5_____

VIDEO GAMES AT HOME

If you're a loyal arcade player, you may turn your back on home video games. They're less exciting, less challenging, you figure.

That may have been true in the past, but not any more. Today's home video games deliver all the excitement you can ask for. At the same time, they give your skills a severe test.

Home video games are improving all the time. In the years ahead they promise to be even more sophisticated and challenging than their arcade cousins.

Home video games have certain built-in advantages. You can play whenever you want to and you never have to leave your living room; you can play all day, and it won't cost you a single quarter.

There are two basic types of home video games. There's the TV hook-up type, explained in this chapter. Then there are hand-held and table-model games. These are examined in the next chapter.

TV hook-up games cost from $150 to $300. For

this, you get an adapter that screws into the VHF-aerial terminal of your television set, and you get the hand controls to play the games. Each unit comes with instructions for attachment.

You then buy a memory cartridge for each game. If you've purchased an Atari adapter and controls, you must make your game selection from the Atari family of cartridges. Cartridges cost from $25 to $50 apiece. Each company has several dozen cartridges available and they keep adding to their stock.

There are five companies that offer home video games. They are:

Atari VCS (Video Computer System)
Intellivision
Odyssey^2
ActiVision
Channel F

Which one is the best system for you? It depends on many factors.

Visit a store that sells games and compare different systems. Check control units. The hand controller for Intellivision games, for instance, has sixteen different positions and four buttons. This means that you can maneuver Intellivision's players and objects in many different directions. Some other control systems provide for only simple player movements.

Also check whether the hand-control unit can be used with all of the company's games. Some game systems require the purchase of additional controllers. This means added expense.

Be sure to check out the assortment of cartridges each company offers. If you're going to be spending most of your time playing the games by yourself, then you'll want to buy cartridges that provide opportunity for solitaire play. On the other hand, if there are always going to be people waiting for a turn at the controls, then you should consider games that permit a number of individuals to play at the same time.

Pick out the system that offers you the widest selection of the kind of games you prefer. For instance, Intellivision offers a great variety of sports games. There's baseball, football, basketball, tennis, ice hockey, and soccer, and also bowling and billiards.

Atari and Odyssey^2 are noted for the many games that first became popular in the arcades. These include Asteroids, Pac-Man, Breakout, Space Invaders, Missile Command, and most of the others.

But don't expect the home video version of your favorite game to be exactly the same as the arcade version. There will be less sound and the graphics are not likely to be as elaborate. In Space Invaders, for example, you're confronted with 55 aliens when you play in an arcade, but the home version has only 36 aliens.

On the other hand, the home version offers several different skill-levels. You can summon up invisible invaders, curving missiles, and other such variations.

The subject of graphics is very important. The term graphics refers to what you see on the screen. With some systems, the graphics are merely symbols. With others, there's a real effort to reproduce the visuals of the game being played.

This applies mainly to sports games. In ice hockey, for example, it's a lot more fun to control skaters that look like hockey players on a rink with goals and all the official markings than to move some X's and O's around against an unmarked background.

The pages that follow report on each of the companies manufacturing and distributing home video games.

Atari VCS
(Video Computer System)

Atari produced Pong, the first big success among coin-operated video games. That was during the mid-1970s. Since that time, the company has held its Number 1 position in video games for both the home and arcades.

Atari's ruggedly built game console is fitted with a heavy-duty plastic case. There are connections for two joysticks or four paddles. Changing from one type of control system to another takes only seconds.

Atari offers a greater assortment of cartridges

than any other company. They're of every type: board and arcade games, strategy and dexterity games, and solitaire and head-to-head contests. Some titles are programmed to provide more than 100 game variations.

Since Atari is the leader in coin-operated games, it should come as no surprise that the company is also out in front in providing home versions of those games. Atari offers cartridges for Asteroids, Missile Command, Space Invaders, Pac-Man, Defender, and Galaxian.

Breakout, the tried and proven ball-and-paddle arcade game, in which you blast away at brick walls, demolishing them one brick at a time, is another Atari cartridge. It includes a raft of variations, a number of which are presented under the title Breakthrough. In these, each time the ball caroms off your paddle, it cuts right through the wall. It takes time to get used to this feature.

Air-Sea Battle has been described as one of the best cartridges in the Atari lineup. In one of this game's variations, opposing players fire at passing ships, competing against each other and against the clock.

Superman is another Atari offering. In this, the "man of steel" pursues Lex Luthor and his evil gang, who have just destroyed the Metropolis Bridge. The game program includes a pesky helicopter, X-ray vision, and kryptonite bombs. Even Lois Lane makes an appearance. The challenge is to make the right move at the right time in a race against the clock.

Atari offers a wide range of traditional favorites, such as chess and checkers. With some of these games, as many as four can play. But the cartridges also give you the option of playing solitaire.

Intellivision

A division of Mattel Electronics, the well-known toy manufacturer (the Barbie Doll is one of its products), Intellivision has made team sports its specialty. NFL Football, Major League Baseball, and NASL Soccer are among its best-known games.

Intellivision offers a superior control system. It is made up of a 12-button keypad and a direction knob to control player movement. These enable you to give a large amount of instructions to the players you command, which adds to each game's drama and excitement.

Intellivision games get high marks for their realism. The baseball game takes place on a simulated diamond. With bowling and soccer, you command humanoid athletes, not symbols. With the golf game, you choose from each of nine different clubs before taking your shot.

Many of the games are extremely sophisticated. In fact, once you become skilled in a particular game, it may be difficult for you to find an opponent who will be able to offer you decent competition.

NBA Basketball not only offers shooting, passing, and shot-blocking, but there are also cheering crowds in the stands. In NHL Hockey there are penalties for breaking the rules. But if you manage to get in a whack while the referee's back is turned, you're likely to get away with it. Auto Racing is not merely one of those around-and-around-and-around-the-oval contests. There is a wide choice of cars and tracks. You can even handicap the better drivers, making each race more hotly contested.

PBA Bowling and Boxing are among the newest additions to the Intellivision family. In the bowling game, you first select a ball of proper weight and decide upon alley slickness. The game furnishes the sound of a ball rolling down the lane and keeps score for you. It can be played by from one to four persons.

Boxing is a two-player game. You control a humanoid boxer who can jab, punch, and feint like Sugar Ray Leonard.

In the past year or so, Intellivision has been improving its line of action games with such offerings as Astrosmash and Triple Action. In Astrosmash, you must vaporize different types of debris that come raining out of the night sky. Triple Action is just that—a three-mode game. It offers tank warfare, air combat, and auto racing. In the air-combat mode, you pilot a rickety World War I biplane. It takes plenty of practice. You're sure to be involved in countless dives and spins that end in flaming death before you can begin to consider yourself an ace.

Odyssey²

The original Odyssey, produced by the Magnavox Company, was the first video game system offered to consumers. But despite its head start, the system was never a success. Magnavox went back to the drawing board and tried again. Odyssey² is the result.

You control Odyssey² games with an electronic keyboard, something like a typewriter keyboard, and two joysticks. No extra hand controls or other keyboard attachments are needed. The keyboard can be used to program different game variations, time limits, and skill-levels.

Odyssey² has a wide variety of cartridges available. There are challenging versions of baseball, golf, and other sports. Computer Golf is one of the best of all the sports-game cartridges. You and your opponent compete on a nine-hole course. When you tee off, you're presented with an overall view of the fairway, complete with an assortment of hazards. Once you're on the green and ready to putt, the scene shifts to a screen that represents the area around the cup.

You use the joystick in selecting the ball's direction. An action button allows you to regulate the force of the stroke.

Odyssey²'s Baseball is also outstanding. Not only does it offer pitching, hitting, running, and fielding in proper balance, the cartridge also allows you to select pitches, move outfielders for defensive reasons, and stretch hits for extra bases.

Odyssey² has put out some rather unusual strategy games. What makes them unusual is that they require not only the planning and maneuvering common to the standard strategy game, but also the dexterity and quick thinking of an action game.

Quest for the Rings is one such game. To win, a pair of heroes must find and capture each of ten magic rings which the leader of the forces of evil has hidden in labyrinths deep beneath the earth. Throughout their quest, the champions of good must outwit and outmaneuver an array of menacing monsters. These include orcs and ogres, vampires and fire-breathing dragons. The graphics are so exciting that many new players surrender outright the first few times they play, just to be able to watch the monsters romp about the screen.

If you're a fan of nonelectronic role-playing games, you'll like Quest for the Rings. Rather than compete directly against the other players, you must cooperate with them in order to achieve victory.

You can also obtain arcade-type games from Odyssey². With these, it's possible for high scorers to post their names on the screen, just as they're able to do in the arcades.

ActiVision

A relatively new company, having been founded in 1980, ActiVision produces no game system of its own; instead, the firm sells game cartridges that are used with the Atari system. Although Acti-Vision hasn't been around for very long, its cartridges have already won applause for their originality and excellent cartoon-style graphics.

Kaboom! is one of ActiVision's most noted games. In this, a mad bomber drops explosives from the top of a wall. Your task is to catch them in fast-moving water buckets before they can explode. One or two can play.

ActiVision also offers sports games. One of them is Tennis. It recreates an actual tennis game in realistic fashion, the ball rocketing back and forth over across the net. So great is the emphasis on realism that the ball even creates a shadow as it flies through the air. Tennis is for one or two players.

Some of ActiVision's games have a humorous touch. In Freeway, for example, the idea is to try to guide a chicken across a busy highway. And in Fishing Derby, opposing anglers attempt to hook underwater targets as they swim back and forth. A shark, who's always ready to gulp down a player's catch, adds fun and excitement.

Channel F

Channel F, like Magnavox, was one of the first

companies to offer a commercial video game system. Also, like Magnavox with Odyssey, the company experienced serious growing pains. The Zircon Company now produces cartridges for the Channel F system.

Channel F offers a decent selection of solitaire games and electronic board games. But it has only a limited number of arcade games and sports games available.

Channel F's Video Whizball is loads of fun. You and your opponent each control a paddle that moves up and down in front of a goal on either side of a playing field. Instead of blocking shots with the paddle, you use it to fire whizballs at a big, floating block, trying to nudge it into your opponent's goal.

The fun increases when a second block appears on the screen, and then a third, and finally a fourth. By that time real havoc has been created.

Channel F's Slot Machine is what you'd expect. The picture of a one-armed bandit dominates the screen. When you use your controls to "pull the handle," the machine's three windows display the familiar pieces of fruit, revealing whether you've won or lost.

Chapter 6

HAND-HELD AND TABLE-MODEL GAMES

Hand-held and table-model games are sometimes called self-contained games. There's no hooking them up to your living room TV. There are no cords and wires. Everything needed to play is housed within the game's case.

As this suggests, you do need batteries. The subject of batteries is discussed later in this chapter.

There are so many hundreds of hand-held and table-model games now available it would take a book the size of this one just to describe them all. Some are very simple, requiring little skill; others are complicated, even too complicated. Prices vary greatly. Indeed, the price for a game can be twice as much in one store as in another.

This means that it's not wise to buy the first game that appeals to you. Look around.

Here are some questions to ask yourself before making a buying decision:

- Is it really an "electronic" game? Some low-priced games are not. They are merely mechanical games with a flashing light or two to indicate a player has scored, and perhaps a buzzer to signal that someone's playing time has expired. An electronic game contains a programmed microprocessor chip, which is in effect a miniature computer. The chip acts as an opposing player.

- Is the game clever and challenging? Will you still be enjoying it after weeks of use? Many games have different skill levels. After you've mastered the game at one level, you can adjust it to a higher level or faster speed.

- How many people can play the game? In virtually every electronic game, you match wits with the computer. But many games have keyboard controls that permit as many as four players to compete against each other as well as the computer.

- How realistic is the game? In the case of a sports-based game, does it simulate on-the-field action?

- Are the game instructions clear and well organized? If they're not, you may have to put in a great deal of time and effort into first learning how to play the game.

- Is the game durable? Watch out for knobs that can get lost or parts that can break off. The game should be sturdy enough to withstand rough treatment.

- What is promised by the game's warranty? You should be able to return the game for a refund if it proves defective, or have it repaired free of charge, within a reasonable time after purchase.

Be sure to play the game before you buy. The store should have a demonstration model available. You want to be sure the game delivers all the thrills and excitement promised by the advertising.

Typical Games

Hand-held and table-model games take several forms and have countless themes. There are warfare games and follow-the-leader games. There are board games and card-and-chance games. There are games for every popular sport, and even for some that aren't so popular. There are educational games. Here's a small sampling of what's available:

World Championship Baseball *(Mattel)*—Videoland offers so many hand-held baseball games it's difficult to keep track of them all. World Championship Baseball is one of the best. Its computer chip is even smarter than Intellivision's Major League Baseball. You can execute double plays and perform pick-off plays at the bases. It even figures "lefty-versus-righty" percentages and makes pitchers tire in the late innings. You get a roster of 15 players before the game begins, and then make up your lineup after weighing their merits as hitters and fielders.

Speak and Spell *(Texas Instruments)*—The microprocessor chip in this clever game duplicates the human voice in helping you to improve your ability to spell. For instance, the voice will ask you how to spell the word *force*. You then press the game's letter keys. "That's correct," the game declares, "now spell calf." If you press the wrong keys the voice advises, "Wrong, try again." A second mistake and the voice takes on the role of a teacher. "That is incorrect," it says, "the correct spelling is *c-a-l-f*." At the same time, the word appears on the Speak and Spell screen.

Speak and Spell comes with a built-in list of some 150 words and a dozen or so additional cartridges. Speak and Read and Speak and Math are other games in the series.

Galaxian 2 *(Entex)*—Many self-contained games attempt to reproduce the action of an arcade model. Galaxian 2 is one of the better efforts. The game's theme is similar to that of Space Invaders, except that the enemy aliens seek to dive-bomb your base in addition to firing from afar. You can play the game by yourself or allow a friend to act as the commander-in-chief of the alien attack.

Simon *(Milton Bradley)*—Introduced in 1978, Simon has threatened to become to hand-held electronic games what Monopoly is to board games. It takes the form of a 12-inch saucer, about three inches high, with colored buttons that send out distinctive musical tones.

Simon works like this: It blinks and blips out a sequence—say: red, yellow, yellow, blue, red, blue, red—and then you try to duplicate it. There are many different skill-levels. As many as four can play. Besides the standard model, there are now pocket-sized and "super" versions. Young children are particularly fond of the game, but if you're an arcade hero, you could tire of it within a week.

Computer Chess *(Mattel)*—This is a screen (not a board) game, which offers four different levels of difficulty, from beginner to champion. You can play either against the computer or watch the computer play itself. It's especially recommended for chess beginners.

Dungeons and Dragons *(Mattel)*—This, of course, is the electronic version of the well-known game of strategy and imagination. The object is to weave your way through a tricky maze to reach a treasure, then rush the prize back to safety with a dragon in hot pursuit. The computer plays the role of the dragon, matching wits with you on the 64-space board.

Quiz Wiz Challenger *(Coleco)*—There are two ways to play this question-and-answer game. In the first version, any player who correctly answers a question scores points. The second version is a race against time, and only the first person answering correctly gets points. As many as four can play. Dozens of different cartridges are available, offering a wide range of topics, from sports to math, from the Bible to Sherlock Holmes.

Dark Tower *(Milton Bradley)*—Warriors battle bands of no-goods, suffer bouts of plague, and search creaking tombs for the magical keys to the tower. Actions depicting game developments are displayed on the tower each time a player takes a turn.

Dallas *(Mattel)*—You get the opportunity to match wits with that scoundrel, J. R. Ewing, in this electronic board game. It's not easy. J. R., as you probably realize, cheats. As many as six people can play, and each takes on the role of one of the Dallas characters. Equipment to play the game includes 24 blackmail cards.

Complaint Department

If you pay $50 to $150 for an electronic game, you expect it to last. But sometimes problems occur. When a game doesn't work right, first contact the store from which you purchased it, then the manufacturer. (Be sure to keep the sales slip, the original carton, and the operating instructions; they'll make it easier for you to get your money back.) If you have difficulty with the manufacturer, write to:

Sally Browne
Consumer Complaint Department
Electronic Industries Association
2000 I St., N.W.
Washington, DC 20006

Ms. Browne will help you to get things straightened out.

All About Batteries

While hand-held and table-model games will never gobble up any of your quarters, they still can cost you money in terms of what you have to pay for batteries.

The best way to keep costs at a minimum is to use batteries of the right type. Electronic games run on either the 9-volt transistor battery or a series of 1.5-volt AA batteries. There are four types:

Carbon-Zinc—These are inexpensive, all-purpose batteries, the kind commonly used in flashlights.

Zinc-Chloride—Known as heavy-duty batteries, these cost a little bit more than the carbon-zinc type, but perform better.

Alkaline—These cost about twice as much as

the zinc-chlorides, but they last much longer.

Nickel-Cadmium—Ni-Cads, as they're called, cost three to four times more than the alkalines. They aren't as easy to find as the other kinds. Try camera shops and electronics stores. Ni-Cads perform steadily, then stop cold. They can be recharged. A recharger costs from $12 to $15. You can recharge a Ni-Cad up to 1,000 times.

This handy chart with figures supplied by Everready, shows that either carbon-zinc or zinc-chloride batteries are likely to be your best buy:

TYPE		Carbon-Zinc	Zinc-Chloride	Alkaline	Nickel-Cadmium
1.5 volt	Cost	$ .4	$ .5	$ 1.1	$4.5
AA	Hours use	7.8	10.1	18.4	6.2
	Cents per hr.	5.8	5.7	6.0	▪
9 volt	Cost	$ 1.0	$ 1.6	$ 2.8	$9.9
	Hours use	10.1	13.6	17.6	3.3
	Cents per hr.	10.3	11.7	16.2	▪

▪ rechargeable

When you buy batteries, be sure to shop around. Not all stores charge the same prices. Some offer big discounts. Never purchase more than a six-month supply.

Store your surplus batteries in the refrigerator. If you plan to keep them more than three months, store them in the freezer in sealed wrap. Be sure to bring them to room temperature before you put them into use.

Some games are equipped with a warning light or give off a beeping sound as a reminder that you've left the game on and are draining the batteries. If you tend to be careless, buy games with this feature.

Another good way to save on batteries is by using an AC adapter. An adapter allows you to plug the game into an ordinary household electric socket without damage to the game's electronics.

An adapter costs about $10. You may find that it pays for itself in a short time.

There are many different types of adapters, however. One type has a fitting that hooks into the game's battery terminals. Another type plugs into a special jack in the game case. Be sure to check the game instructions so you buy the right type.

Chapter 7 _____

A VIDEO GAME QUIZ

The twelve questions that make this quiz are meant to test your knowledge of electronic video games and how they're played. The answers are given after Question 12.

If you get only four or fewer answers right, you're assigned to go back and read this book from the beginning. Get five or six correct, and you probably still think Scramble is a way to prepare eggs; seven or eight correct, the chances are good that you've gotten as far as halftime in Pac-Man at least once or twice; nine or ten right, you may be spending too much time in the arcades; and eleven or twelve right, you should be thinking about moving to Sunnyvale, California. Atari and some of those other game companies will want to hire you.

1. A particular video game was once so popular in Japan that it caused a yen shortage because so many millions upon millions of the coins were locked away in machines. That game was:

A. Asteroids
B. Space Invaders
C. Breakout

2. Steve Juraszek, 15, of Arlington Heights, Illinois, once played Defender for 16 hours and 34 minutes on the same quarter. What was Steve's score?

A. 6,782,700
B. 11,289,800
C. 15,963,100

3. When Nolan Bushnell formed his own company to produce video games and was choosing a name for it, he borrowed a term from the Japanese game of Go and called his firm Atari. Atari means:

A. "I'm sorry."
B. "Your turn."
C. "Prepare to be attacked."

4. Berzerk, Astro-Blaster, and Vanguard all have one thing in common. What is it?

A. Each is a maze game.
B. Each involves a humanoid.
C. Each has the power of speech.

5. George Brett of the Kansas City Royals was the American League's Most Valuable Player in 1980. Mike Schmidt of the Philadelphia Phillies was named the National League's MVP that same

year. During the baseball strike in 1981, Mattel brought the two together for a game of video baseball. Who won?

6. Everyone knows that more boys than girls play video games. Of all arcade users, what percentage are males (according to *Newsweek* magazine):

    A. Ninety percent
    B. Eighty percent
    C. Seventy percent

7. In 1980, a federal appeals court ruled as illegal a law that prohibited anyone under 17 years of age to play arcade video games without permission of their parents. That law was passed by the town of:

    A. Mesquite, Texas
    B. Springfield, Massachusetts
    C. Skokie, Illinois

8. In 1982, *Electronic Games* magazine polled its readers to determine the most popular home video game. According to the survey, the Number 1 hit was:

    A. Baseball (Intellivision)
    B. UFO (Odyssey²)
    C. Asteroids (Atari VCS)

9. If you're a computer freak, you'll know that the part of a computer that permits the attachment of a joystick, firing button, or even a cas-

sette recorder, is called:

    A. An interpreter
    B. An interface
    C. A mode

10. One country of the world, describing the video game as a "social enemy" and an "electrical bandit," has outlawed its use. That country is:

    A. The Philippines
    B. Canada
    C. South Africa

11. You can buy the Midway Manufacturing Corporation arcade version of Pac-Man and set it up in your bedroom. All it takes is:

    A. $3,000
    B. $5,800
    C. $12,000

12. Pac-Man fans have created several nicknames for the game's characters and its various features. Match each of the terms in the column on the left with its correct nickname.

    A. Pac-Man   1. Killer Pill
    B. Energizer   2. Zombies
    C. Monsters   3. The Tube
    D. Tunnel   4. Jaws

Answers

1. B
2. C
3. C
4. C
5. Schmidt. He trounced Brett by the lopsided score of 31–7.
6. A
7. A
8. C
9. B
10. A
11. A
12. A–4
    B–1
    C–2
    D–3

Chapter 8

GREAT DATES IN VIDEO GAMES

Nolan Bushnell. His name should be ranked with Thomas Edison's and Alexander Graham Bell's, according to some people. Bushnell was the inventor of the first coin-operated video game.

Bushnell got the video game idea while he was an engineering student at the University of Utah. But he didn't start developing it until 1969.

At that time Bushnell was a research engineer for Ampex, a company best known for making recording tape. After working all day, Bushnell would return to his small house in Santa Clara, California, and work on his game. He did his designing in his daughter's bedroom. "I kicked her out," he says. "She had to double up with my other daughter."

Bushnell finished drawing up plans for the world's first video game in 1971. A flying saucer battled a rocket ship. Bushnell called the game Computer Space.

Computer Space was a flop. Only 2,000 were

sold. All of Bushnell's friends loved the game, but all of Bushnell's friends were engineers. "I decided a simpler game was needed," he says.

After more hard work, Bushnell developed a video version of Ping-Pong, which he named Pong. Electronic paddles slapped a ball back and forth across a black-and-white TV screen. You could play another person or the game could play you.

Bushnell put Pong in a tavern in Sunnyvale, California, to see whether anyone would pay to play it. A few days later, Bushnell got a call from the owner of the tavern saying that the game had broken down.

Bushnell went to investigate. He quickly found out what was wrong. Pong was filled to overflowing with money, literally choking to death on quarters. Bushnell knew immediately that he had a success on his hands.

At the time that Bushnell was toiling away on the design of Pong, another engineer, named Ralph Baer, had already started work on a device that would enable a person to play electronic games on home television. Baer and his associates developed video hockey and Ping Pong, producing images on a 17-inch RCA color TV set.

In 1972, the same year that Nolan Bushnell was testing Pong in the California tavern, the Magnavox Company introduced Ralph Baer's home video game system, called Odyssey.

The year 1972 thus stands as a landmark year in the brief history of video games. Here are some other important dates:

1975

Coleco introduces Telestar Arcade, the first notable hand-held game. By Christmas 1976, more than 70 companies are providing hand-held video games for the home market.

1976

Nolan Bushnell sells his company, Atari, to Warner Communications for $28 million. Before long, Bushnell is involved in a new venture, the Chuck E. Cheese Pizza Time Theaters. Each theater is part pizza parlor, part video entertainment center.

1976

Atari introduces Breakout. You attempt to knock a hole in a brick wall so you can escape from jail. It's great fun. Some 15,000 games are sold. Breakout is the Number 1 game of the year.

1977

A "Gametronic Conference," bringing together all of the leading personalities in the video game field, is held in San Francisco. Awards are given to Nolan Bushnell and Ralph Baer for their contributions as video game pioneers.

1978

Taito Corporation, a Japanese manufacturer, creates Space Invaders, the first big video game hit. Midway Division of the Bally Corporation is licensed to make the arcade version. The game starts showing up in airports, candy stores, delicatessens, gas stations, supermarkets, Chinese restaurants—everywhere.

Your task in Space Invaders is to destroy the alien invaders before they destroy you. You have a laser base from which you shoot and four shelters that offer protection against the advancing bomb-slinging attackers.

The game is something of a tease. You're made to believe that it will take only a few more tries to wipe out the first wave of attackers. Says one player, "You can get good—great, even—but you'll never totally beat it. Space Invaders plays with your mind."

1979

Late in the year, Atari introduces Asteroids. It quickly becomes the hottest game in town.

Asteroids looks as though it's quite simple to play. The player controls a triangular spaceship that dodges big rocks or blasts away at them, shattering them into smaller rocks that also must be avoided or destroyed. Occasionally an enemy spaceship comes orbiting by, firing away. There are bonus points for shooting it down.

But Asteroids offers unusual features. The player's spaceship can rotate 360 degrees, and it can zoom at different speeds in all directions.

Asteroids is the first game to appeal to adults as well as kids. "When you play the game, the rest of

the world ceases to exist," says one man. "You
can't even hear what's going on around you. People
could be breaking chairs over each other's
heads and you wouldn't move."

1980

Video magazine establishes the Arcade Awards—
called Arkies—to recognize outstanding achievements
in the video game field. They're similar to
the Oscars, which the movie industry awards each
year, and to television's Emmys. Arkie winners
for 1980 include:

Best Arcade Game: Space Invaders *(Taito)*
Most Innovative Game: Basketball *(Atari)*
Best Sports Game: Football *(Professional
Arcade)*
Best Target Game: Air-Sea Battle *(Atari)*
Best Science-Fiction Game: Cosmic Conflict
(Odyssey²)
Best Solitaire Game: Gold *(Odyssey²)*

1980

Mattel launches its game-playing computer,
Intellivision.

1980

Pac-Man makes its debut. Manufactured by Midway,
Pac-Man is a hide-and-seek game that has to
do with eating fruit, gobbling dots, and avoiding
monsters.

It is the first video game to appeal to females.
Within a year after its introduction, more than 4

billion quarters are pumped into Pac-Man. It becomes the most popular video game ever.

1980

ActiVision, the first company to provide cartridges for other firms' consoles, is formed.

1981

Arkie award winners are as follows:

Best Arcade Game: Asteroids *(Atari)*
Most Innovative Game: Adventure *(Atari)*
Game of the Year: Superman *(Atari)*
Best Sports Game: NASL Soccer *(Mattel)*
Best Target–War Game: Armored Battle *(Atari)*
Best Science-Fiction Game: Space Battle *(Mattel)*
Best Solitaire Game: Skiing *(ActiVision)*
Best Audio-Visual Effects: Fishing Derby *(ActiVision)*

1981

Electronic Games, the first magazine devoted exclusively to the video game field, comes into existence.

1982

Arkie awards, co-sponsored by *Video* and *Electronic Games* magazines, are as follows:

Video Game of the Year: Asteroids *(Atari)*
Best Arcade Game: Pac-Man *(Namco/Midway)*
Most Innovative Game: Quest for the Rings *(Odyssey²)*
Best Competitive Game: Tennis *(ActiVision)*

Best Solitaire Game: Missile Command *(Atari)*

Best Science-Fiction Game: UFO *(Odyssey²)*

Best Sports Game: USAC Auto Racing *(Mattel)*

Best Audio-Visual Effects: Kaboom *(ActiVision)*

Computer Game of the Year: Star Raiders *(Atari)*

Best Computer Action Game: Jawbreaker *(On-Line)*

Best Computer Sports Game: Computer Baseball *(Strategic Simulations)*

Best Computer Adventure: Empire of the Over-Mind *(Avalon-Hill)*

What's ahead? More games, of course. And games that challenge more.

You're going to see more gobble games on the order of Pac-Man and Ms. Pac-Man. Midway, the company that brought you those games, is releasing Kick-Man, hoping it gains a fraction of the popularity achieved by the Pacs.

You'll see more talking games, such as Berzerk. There are going to be voice-activated games in which you give verbal instructions to the computer. Three-dimensional games are also on the way.

Other games of the future will be able to be manned by as many as four players. They'll blast away at one another until only one player survives for final combat with the computer.

Some news isn't good. In some parts of the United States, the 50-cent game is already a reality. And the dollar game is being talked about.

Many different uses are being found for video games. The army is using a slightly altered version of Battlezone as a training device. The medical school at Johns Hopkins University uses special Atari games to determine the effects of certain medicines on the human nervous system. The Capital Children's Museum in Washington, D.C., uses a video game to teach young children about computers.

Video games have been around for only about ten years, and look at the impact they've had. The next ten years promise to be even more exciting.